Studies in Philosophy and Religion

GENERAL EDITOR: P. R. BAELZ

Regius Professor of Moral and Pastoral Theology
University of Oxford

Contemporary interest in religion is widespread. The interpretation of man's religious experience raises fundamental questions of knowledge and truth to which philosophical analysis and reflection are highly relevant. The present series will include a variety of writings which explore the significance and validity of the claims of religion to give insight into the reality of the world and God.

Studies in Philosophy and Religion

TRUTH AND DIALOGUE

The Relationship between World Religions

EDITED BY

JOHN HICK

SHELDON PRESS
LONDON

First published
in Great Britain in 1974
by Sheldon Press Marylebone Road
London NW1 4DU

Copyright © 1974 University of Birmingham

Printed in Great Britain by
Northumberland Press Limited
Gateshead

ISBN 0 85969 012 1

Contents

Acknowledgements

Thanks are due to the following for permission to quote from copyright sources:

Christian Institute for the Study of Religion and Society: an article by C. Murray Rogers in *Religion and Society* (March 1965); 'Preparation for Dialogue' by H. J. Singh from *Inter-Religious Dialogue* ed. H. J. Singh

The Christian Literature Society: *The Church in India* by Abhishiktananda

Curtis Brown Ltd: *Questions of Religious Truth* by W. Cantwell Smith

Macmillan Publishing Company Inc: 'Concensus, Conflict and Co-operation' by I. L. Horowitz in *System, Change and Conflict* ed. Demerath and Pearson

Routledge & Kegan Paul Ltd: *Answer to Job* by C. G. Jung

Editor's Preface

This book is a product of a Conference on the Philosophy of Religion held in April 1970 under the auspices of the Department of Theology at the University of Birmingham with the aid of a grant from the Edward Cadbury Trust. The aim of the conference was to discuss the relation between world religions in view of their apparently conflicting truth-claims.

The participants in the conference were Professor Robert Adams and Dr Marilyn Adams of the Department of Philosophy in the University of Michigan; Professor Christian Baeta of the Department of Religion in the University of Ghana; Mr John Bowker of Corpus Christi College, Cambridge; Dr Jehangir Chubb, formerly Professor and head of the Department of Philosophy at Elphinstone College, University of Bombay, India; Professor Gordon Davies, Mr Daniel Hardy, and Professor John Hick of the Department of Theology at Birmingham University; Professor Trevor Ling of the Department of Comparative Religion at Manchester University; Professor Geoffrey Parrinder of the Department of the History and Philosophy of Religion at King's College, London; Professor Santosh Sengupta of the Centre for the Advanced Study of Philosophy, Visva-Bharati, Santiniketan, India; Dr Eric Sharpe and Professor Ninian Smart of the Department of Religious Studies at the University of Lancaster; Professor Wilfred Cantwell Smith, then head of the Centre for the Study of World Religions at Harvard University; Dr John Taylor of the Selly Oak Colleges, Birmingham; and Professor R. C. Zaehner of All Souls College, Oxford. Bishop Kenneth Cragg of Jerusalem was a corresponding member.

I should like to record gratitude to the Trustees of the Edward Cadbury Trust, whose grant made it possible for the conference to be held; to the British Council for enabling Professor Sengupta to be with us, and to the Centre for the Study of World Religions at Harvard University for assistance with the publication of this book; and to my colleague, Julius Lipner, for reading the proofs.

JOHN HICK

Religious Truth

R. C. ZAEHNER

'I was born for this, I came into the world for this: to bear witness to the truth...' 'Truth?' said Pilate, 'What is that?'; and with that he went out again to the Jews and said, 'I find no case against him.'[1]

Pilate may be taken as the type of an irreligious man. 'Truth', in a religious sense must have seemed to him merely tedious, since in religion what to one man is truth is to another a lie. In any case it is scarcely important enough to take legal action about. Civilized people do not sentence men for their usually quite irrational beliefs. This is a pagan attitude and is dominant in Western Europe and North America today. If there is such a thing as religious truth, it is a purely private affair and must not be allowed to interfere with the good government of society. The religious man, on the other hand, at least in the Near East, felt quite differently: hence Caiaphas's reactions to Jesus' claims are the exact opposite of Pilate's.

The high priest put a second question to him, 'Are you the Christ,' he said, 'the Son of the Blessed One?' 'I am,' said Jesus ... The high priest tore his robes, 'What need of witness have we now? You heard the blasphemy.'[2]

Caiaphas was a Jew; and for him religious truth mattered very much indeed. To claim to be the Son of God was blasphemy and a challenge to the central Jewish dogma of the absolute oneness of God. This is an attitude typical both of Judaism and of her daughter religion Islam. It is not typical of Indian and Chinese religions, and even so broadminded and cultured a Muslim as Al-Bīrūnī was amazed at what seemed to him the indifference of the Hindus to religious truth.

'They totally differ from us in religion,' he wrote, 'as we believe in nothing in which they believe and *vice versa*. On the whole, there is very little disputing about theological topics among themselves; at the utmost, they fight with words, but they will never stake their soul or body or their property on religious controversy.'[3]

It is superfluous to repeat once again that historically the predominantly mystical religions of India have a far cleaner record in the matter of persecution than have the prophetic religions of the Near East. But why this should be so is not quite so easy to determine. Nobody talks more about the Truth than the mystics, and yet it is they who seem to be most indifferent to the spread of the 'truth' as they experience it. Certainly there has been friction between Hindus and Buddhists in India as there has been between Buddhists and Confucians in China, but the concept of a 'holy war', whether it be the war of extermination waged by the Hebrews against the Canaanites, or the Muslim *jihād*, or the Christian Crusade, is quite foreign to Indian and Chinese religion. When the Confucians persecuted the Buddhists in China, it was not on account of their particular attitude to 'truth' but because their beliefs resulted in undesirable *practices*, the disruption of family life which was the cornerstone on which the Confucian ethic rested. Buddhism, from the Confucian point of view, was disruptive of the established society: it was an anti-social force.

In an earlier book I distinguished between the prophetic and mystical 'types' of religion. By and large this distinction seems to be valid. Mystical religion is concerned with discovering eternity within you: it cannot be communicated directly to others except through long association of master and disciple: it is not and cannot be a public affair, and in any case the mystic is not concerned with the regulation of the affairs of *this* world, but in transcending the world and entering into a totally different and unconditioned form of existence beyond the whole realm of time and space. Prophecy, on the other hand, claims to be a direct communication from a highly personal God who is experienced as an *outside* power who has a direct and pressing message to deliver to a religious community or indeed to all mankind through the prophet in this world of space and time.

Among the great religions of mankind a further distinction can be made: on the one hand you have religions that stress individual salvation; on the other, religions in which the 'salvation' of the community takes precedence over that of the individual. On the whole, religions of 'solidarity' tend to coalesce with prophecy, while religions in which the individual is stressed tend to be mystical. The exception is Confucianism, for neither Confucius nor Mencius can be regarded as prophets in the sense that the Old Testament prophets and Muhammad were. True, they speak of the will of heaven and the mandate of heaven and they claim to interpret them; but their message is one of restoring a lost harmony in purely human terms. 'God' or 'heaven' is not clearly distinguished from nature: he or it never wholly transends it as Yahweh and Allah do.

But whether religions are 'solidary' or 'solitary', they all make claims to truth. Is it at all possible to reconcile these various 'truths'? On the prophetic side it is indeed difficult to see how this can be done: on the mystical side it is very much less so, as is obvious from the great majority of writers on mysticism, who tend to treat mystical experience as an identical phenomenon with a wide variety of interpretations. To this we shall have to return.

For the moment, however, we shall have to consider the nature of the sacred books of the various religions. Here the first thing that strikes one is – with the single exception of the Qur'ān – how very haphazard their composition seems to have been. And even the Qur'ān cannot be said to be coherently arranged, nor are its contents (as Muslims themselves will admit) equally inspired. For instance Sūra 111 ('May the hands of Abū Lahab perish ...') can scarcely be said to rank as an expression of religious truth of the same order as the following Sūra ('Say: He is God, the One, God, the Eternal ...'). This we will find in all sacred books. Each contains a kernel that is of central importance to the believer, but also a mass of material that is, in practice, expendable. The difficulty, of course, is that the vital core is different in all religions.

In recent times the Neo-Vedāntins have put forward the thesis that the inmost core of all religions is the same, that each of the religions is a path leading to this identical goal and is therefore valid as an approach. Once you have ascended to the Truth itself, however, the ladder will have served its purpose and can be disposed of. Similarly, as the Buddhists would say, you use a boat to ferry you across the river of *saṁsāra*, but once you have reached the farther shore, which is Nirvāṇa, you will not carry the boat around with you. This, however, is to assume that mystical religion is alone true and that prophetic religion is and can be only *relatively* true. It is also to assume that mystical experience is the only valid religious experience (because in theory it is open to everyone) while prophetic experience is in some way less authentic because it is vouchsafed to very few and has not the consistency of the mystical variety. To this we may reply that mystical experience of any kind is not at all common, for as the Bhagavad-Gītā (7.3) says: 'Among thousands of men but one, maybe, will strive for self-perfection, and even among Yogins who have won perfection, but one, maybe, will come to know me as I really am.'

For the average human being, faith is the necessary prerequisite to experience, whether he aspires to the beatific vision, the Muslim paradise, the Buddhist Enlightenment, or the Hindu 'liberation'. Hence Uddālaka Āruni, when explaining what is meant by the celebrated *tat tvam asi* ('That you are'), so far from treating this proposition as being self-evident as Neo-Vedāntins are liable to do, says: 'It is true that you cannot perceive this finest essence, but it is equally true that this huge fig-tree grows up from this same finest essence. My dear child, *have faith.*'[4]

If it is true that 'the fear of the Lord is the beginning of wisdom'[5] and if, as the Jerusalem Bible says, 'the fear of the Lord ... is approximately what we call the virtue of religion, or devotion to God', then faith must be the base on which any religious enterprise is founded. But faith in what or whom?

It seems quite clear that the Christian faith is still in rapid decline among the educated classes in the West; and this loss of faith, this loss of any permanent, fixed set of values, is very largely responsible for the disarray so clearly apparent among modern western youth. A minority is looking for a new religion; but the majority is content to ask, like Pilate, 'Truth, what is that?', and the question is rhetorical. These are what Teilhard de Chardin contemptuously dismissed as 'the inert and uninteresting mass of those who believe in nothing'.[6] They now have both bread and circuses in abundance, and that seems to satisfy them. It probably always has done so, since even in the so-called ages of faith it is doubtful whether there was ever more than a small minority to which religion meant anything very much; the average man is a conformist and quite happy to go along with the majority. The difference between the modern age and all preceding ages is that there is no longer any religious or even cultural norm in which man can feel at home. This is obviously true in the West and is in the process of becoming true in the non-Christian civilizations too. Everywhere the educated classes are reacting against religion in general and their own religion in particular. This is particularly true in the traditionally Protestant countries, and for fairly obvious reasons.

Medieval Catholicism was still permeated by a living mystical tradition; and what was true of the Catholic Church was also true of the more popular heresies such as the Brethren of the Free Spirit. God was still Emmanuel, 'God-among-us', a God whose presence was felt and with whom one could live on easy terms: he was real. What the Reformation did by so unwisely resuscitating the Old Testament was not only to put God back to where he had been before the incarnation – beyond the firmament – but also to re-present him as the 'Lord God of armies' in all his naked savagery. Such a God might correspond to the temperament of the reformers, fired as they were by a truly 'righteous' indignation; but once the fires of the wars of religion had died down and men began to wonder how they could have torn themselves to pieces for what now seemed irrelevant issues, the Lord God himself ceased to be credible, and in the hands of Voltaire he became merely ridiculous. Already in the eighteenth century the educated classes had ceased to take seriously this Judaeo-Protestant God who was not only a savage but quite out-of-date. Unmitigated transcendentalism had been tried and found wanting. The backlash took longer to make itself felt in North America, but now it has come with a vengeance; and it is precisely in America that an intense interest in the immanentist religions of the East has arisen. Of course there are still advocates of God as the 'wholly other' around, but they are practically all theologians, and theology as practised today is of no interest to secular man, to 'the inert and uninteresting mass of those who believe in nothing'. But is it their fault that they believe in nothing? After all, until quite recently they had been offered so few options, since the god of their fathers had been the God of the Old Testament, the God who drove Aldous Huxley and C. G. Jung out of their respective denominations, making them disillusioned and disgusted men until they, each in his own turn and way, discovered Eastern spirituality. Indeed so strongly did Jung feel that the figure of Yahweh was destructive of any balanced view of the divine that he did his best to psychoanalyse him out of existence in his remarkable little book *Answer to Job*. In justification for writing this violent attack on the Old Testament God he wrote: 'I hope to act as a voice for many who feel the same way as I do, and to give expression to the shattering emotion that the unvarnished spectacle of divine savagery and ruthlessness produces in us.'[7] And this is what Jung has to say about the 'divine savage':

The Book of Job is a landmark in the long historical development of the divine drama. At the time the book was written, there
were already many testimonies which had given a contradictory
picture of Yahweh – the picture of a God who knew no moder-

ation in his emotions and suffered precisely from this lack of moderation. He himself admitted that he was eaten up with rage and jealousy and that this knowledge was painful to him. Insight existed along with obtuseness, loving-kindness along with cruelty, creative power along with destructiveness. Everything was there, and none of these qualities was an obstacle to the other. Such a condition is only thinkable either when no reflecting consciousness is present at all, or when the capacity for reflection is very feeble or a more or less adventitious phenomenon. A condition of this sort can only be described as *amoral*.[8]

These are strong words, but they are scarcely an exaggeration. The God of the Old Testament is what Aurobindo calls a 'bully and a tyrant' and his only excuse is that 'he justifies himself in the end'.[9] The West has to all intents and purposes finished with him. The only valid defence of him is that he had to be represented in these terms to a primitive and savage people. He had to be humanized in the Wisdom books (most of which were rejected by the Jews and Protestants) and again in the Talmud. For the ancient Hebrews he was no doubt an overwhelming and inescapable 'truth'; but since Judaism is essentially a religion that works itself out in time, it is a 'truth' that cannot but supersede itself – religiously speaking, a relative truth.

The Western interest in Eastern religions is very largely a revulsion against this type of deity, what Protestants call the God of history; for if history – and religious history in particular – teaches us anything, it is that every single ideal, whether religious or secular, that man has ever had, is sooner or later utterly corrupted. We seem to be imprisoned in a cycle of *yin* and *yang*, in the *saṁsāra* of cyclic time to which no end can be foreseen. The only answer for the individual, then, is to find eternity within himself. Hence it is Hinduism and Buddhism (and Taoism) that have attracted post-Christian man, not Islam because the Allah of the Qur'ān is in his 'divine savagery' barely distinguishable from Yahweh; and there is a mordant irony in the fact that this God should be fighting himself to the death in Palestine today. It is true that mystical universalists like Frithjof Schuon describe themselves as Muslims, but the Islam they espouse is, of course, a type of Sūfīsm which to the orthodox Muslims is no Islam at all. And yet the tendency among all modernist movements in all religions has been to return to the original scriptures over the head of established religious *traditions.* This was, of course, the battle-cry of classical Protestant-ism as it is of Protestant Neo-Othodoxy. It has also been the leitmotiv of practically all the more recent Muslim reformers as it has been of Dayānanda and Aurobindo among the Hindus, and to a lesser extent among the other Hindu revivalists. Buddhism, as usual, is a special case, and we shall have to consider it later.

And yet religious traditions themselves are highly selective in their treatment of their own sacred books. Each part of the book or books is normally held to be equally sacred, and this may be all very well as a working hypothesis, but in practice it is never true. For the Jews, for instance, the Torah takes precedence over the rest of the Bible, while for the Hindus the Upanishads together with certain creation hymns of the Rig-Veda form the core of revelation with the addition of the Bhagavad-Gītā which does not form part of the sacred canon at all. And this is surprising, for the Gītā represent a departure from the main Upanishadic teaching almost as radical as is that tradition itself from the religion of the *Saṁhitās* and *Brāhmaṇas.* It is not easy to explain this except on the grounds that room had to be made for the increasing importance of the *bhakti* cults that were beginning to claim the allegiance of the masses. And here, I think, there is an important point. Although it is true that religions can most easily be classified as mystical and prophetic, other-worldy and this-worldly, 'solitary' and 'solidary', they are unlikely to survive if one aspect is stressed to the total exclusion of the other. Hence we might almost say that in Budd-hism the Mahāyāna *had* to develop out of the Hīnayāna schools, the *Śvetāśvatara* Upanishad and the Gītā *had* to develop out of the pantheism and monism of the Upanishads, and on the other side the Kabbala *had* to develop out of the legalism of the Talmud, and Sūfism *had* to develop out of the legal and theological aridities of the law-schools and Ash'arite theology in Islam. In all religions, then, we can detect a search for a Middle Way that will make room for both a changeless and ineffable Absolute on the one hand and a God who acts in time (the God of history and ethics) on the other. About the Absolute – what the Upanishads call 'the Real of the Real' or 'the True of the True', there cannot really be much disagreement since you cannot define it except as the 'eternal' – the 'eternal among eternals, conscious among the unconscious, the One among the many'[10], as the 'unborn, not become, not made or compounded'[11], as 'God, the One, God, the Eternal'[12], 'the first and last, the outward and the inward'[13], as 'I am who is'[14]. This much the religions have in common: and this much is everything, and it is nothing; it is the ultimate 'knowledge' of the mystics that is, however, also a 'cloud of unknowing' and an eternal stumbling-block to the non-mystic. For such 'knowledge' is the denial of all empirical knowledge of God as he acts in and influences the world – what is usually called the God of revelation.

Judaism, Christianity, Zoroastrianism, and Islam all profess to tell us not only that God *is* but also *what* he is, how he acts, and what is his relationship to man. They also tell us what should be man's response to this, humanly speaking, amoral being, this *yaksha*, this ' "goblin" possessed of self'[15], 'immortal, wise, and self-existent'[16]. The answer of both the Old Testament and the Qur'ān is total obedience to the commands of this being as revealed by his prophets – however sanguinary these commands may be. This too is part of the message of the Bhagavad-Gītā and, for that matter, of the Zoroastrian *Gāthās*: the 'chosen' people must convert or destroy the 'followers of the Lie' as Zoroaster calls them, the 'idol-worshippers' so abhorrent to the Semitic faiths. For, after all, God is the sole agent; it is he who hardens Pharaoh's heart, and as the Qur'ān (8.17) says, 'You did not slay them, but God slew them; and when thou threwest, it was not thyself that threw but God threw.' So too in the Gītā (11.32-3) Krishna tells Arjuna in no uncertain terms that whether he wants to or not he has no choice but to slay the sons of Dhritarāshtra, for God is the real agent, Arjuna but a tool:

> Do what you will, all these warriors shall cease to be ... And so stand up, win glory, conquer your enemies and win a prosper-ous kingdom! Long since have these men in truth been slain by me: yours it is to be the mere occasion.

Jung is right. In the God of revelation (and this, of course, applies to Śiva too) 'insight exists along with obtuseness, loving-kindness along with cruelty, creative power along with destructive-ness. Everything is there, and none of these qualities is an obstacle to the other.' If God is amoral, why then does he expect man to be moral? As usual the Hindus are very much more realistic than the rest. In the Upanishads God is beyond good and evil, and so the man who has realized his identity with God both as the absolute and as operative in time must be beyond good and evil too. Only the Buddhists and the Zoroastrians could escape from the amorality of God, the first by denying his existence, the second by presupposing an ἀντίτεχνος, a rival artificer, who is either the 'Lie' or, more personally conceived of, the destructive spirit. The God of the Upanishads, insofar as he is personal, is, like Yahweh and Allah, beyond good and evil; and so man, being in some sense identical with God, once he has realized this identity or affinity, is also beyond good and evil: he is beyond conscience. As the devil says to Ivan Karamazov in Dostoievsky's novel: 'There is no law for God. Where God stands, the place is holy. Where I (the 'new man', the 'man-god') stand will at once be the foremost place ... "All things are lawful," and that's the end of it.' So, too, we read in the *Kaushītaki* Upanishad (3.1):

> Indra did not swerve from the truth, for Indra *is* truth. So he said:
>
> 'Know me, then, as I am. This indeed is what I consider most beneficial for mankind – that they should know me. I killed the three-headed son of Tvashtri, I threw the Arunmukha ascetics to the hyenas. Transgressing many a compact, I impaled the people of Prahlāda to the sky, the Paulomas to the atmosphere and the Kālakāñjas to the earth, and I did not lose a single hair in the process.
>
> 'The man who knows me as I am loses nothing that is his, whatever he does, even though he should slay his mother or his father, even though he steal or procure an abortion. Whatever he does, he does not blanch.'

So too, of the man who has realized the Self within him, it is said:

> 'These two thoughts do not occur to him, "So I have done evil", or "So I have done good". He shrugs them off. What he has done and what he has left undone does not torment him ...
>
> 'Hence the man who thus knows will be at peace, tamed, quietly contented, long-suffering, recollected, for he will see the Self in himself: he will see all things as the Self. Evil does not touch him: all evils he shrugs off. Evil does not torment him: all evil he burns out.'[17]

The moral is clear. If God or the Self is beyond good and evil, then the man who 'sees the Self in himself' will, by the mere fact that he has identified himself with this 'goblin possessed of self', have himself passed beyond good and evil.

In Hinduism all this makes sense. 'The absolute is what the Gītā (2.72) calls *brāhmī sthitiḥ*, the *fixed, still* state of Brahman', in which change of any sort is inconceivable. But this 'fixed, still state' is also the source of the phenomenal world – of time, space, and action whether good or evil. God, then, is the sole agent in the phenomenal world. He becomes incarnate to restore *dharma*, but in the course of the *Mahābhārata* in which the Gītā is an episode, he shows himself to be beyond the *dharma* he has himself created and which he professes to restore. The 'righteousness' he demands of men does not apply to himself, and so, during the great war, it is Yudhishthira, the 'king of righteousness' and son of the god Dharma, who upholds *dharma*, not Krishna, who continually infringes. it. Like Yahweh and Allah, Krishna's purposes are inscrutable, and from the purely human point of view he is unjust. This is perhaps why the Buddha refused to admit the existence of an absolute that had any connection with the phenomenal world, for once such a connection is admitted, the absolute is *ipso facto* tainted with and ultimately responsible for evil. For the Buddha there can be no connection between eternal peace and the constant strife that is of the essence of earthly life. There can, then, be no personal God who is responsible for what goes on in the world, and so mystical experience can be interpreted only as an escape from the chronic instability of the world. From the Buddhist point of view the 'God of history' who appoints his prophet 'to tear up and to knock down, to destroy and to overthrow, to build and to plant'[18], can only be Māra, the devil, who is the personification of *saṁsāra*, of birth and death, and desire that is ultimately responsible for the whole ghastly round of existence. But the Buddha's Enlightenment, which entails his complete dissociation from and disgust with the world, is counterbalanced by his compassion for the world that sets in motion the wheel of the Buddhist *dharma* through which, in the course of ages, all men may be saved *from* the world. Salvation means salvation *from* the world, not salvation and sanctification *of* the world: for the world, since it is self-evidently in a state of continual flux, must also be devoid of substance and therefore always subject to an ineradicable disquiet. Hence it is in itself the denial of the eternal and so to speak at war with it.

Basically Hīnayāna Buddhism is the ancestor of Manichaeanism with its fundamental dualism between spirit and matter. By identifying evil with matter it leaves out of account purely spiritual evil: it knows nothing of the Zoroastrian Ahriman. If the Buddhist

ancestry of Manichaeanism is admitted, then it can be said that
Zoroastrianism was at least the midwife to Christianity. Buddhism,
of all the great religions, is perhaps the most rational, and this
accounts for the keen interest it has aroused in the post-Christian
West. Christianity, on the other hand, is perhaps the most irrational
of all the religions, 'to the Jews an obstacle that they cannot get
over, to the pagans madness'[19]. Or, more bluntly, in the words of
Dr Alan Watts: 'Christianity ... impresses the modern Westerner
as the most impossibly complicated amalgamation of odd ideas,
and though it is his spiritual birthright and the faith of his fathers,
it is very much easier to help him understand Buddhism or
Vedānta'[20]. Many teachers of the history of religions will agree. It
is, however, perhaps easier to understand Christianity over against
the background of the non-Christian religions rather than, as here-
tofore, as a Jewish heresy overlaid with Hellenistic ideas. Christianity, so seen, is the reconciliation of the opposites of the 'mystical'
and 'prophetic' religions. Let us, then, consider, one by one, the
various concepts that are present in all the great religions, and see
what the Christian position is when seen over against them.

1. What is the nature of the absolute?

All religions agree that it is One, eternal, beyond space and time.
For the Hindus and Buddhists it is also perfect peace. The Hindus
go further and define it as being, consciousness, and joy. To
'become' the absolute is the ultimate goal of Hinduism and, some
would say, of Buddhism too. This is also the goal of the more
advanced Sūfis in Islam. The absolute *qua* absolute, however,
though it can be discerned in the Qur'ān is not in fact the subject
matter of either orthodox Islam or orthodox Judaism, nor is it of
any interest to the Zoroastrians. It is not considered to be important.

2. What is the nature of God as Person?

In Judaism, Islam, Hinduism, and even in Confucianism (in the
Book of Songs) God is beyond good and evil and the author of both.
His will is arbitrary and unaccountable: he is both compassionate
and terrifying: he is love and he is wrath. In the Old Testament
and the Qur'ān he shows no sort of consistency since he continually
repents of what he has done. Only in Zoroastrianism is he un-
equivocally good, evil arising from a separate principle – Ahriman
or the devil. In Buddhism he does not exist, while in the extreme

form of the non-dualist Vedānta he has no more than illusory existence.

3. What is the nature of man?

(a) Hinduism has no consistent view about this, but at least this much can be said: he is not a unity but an uneasy amalgam of spirit and matter, of the eternal and the transient. Salvation consists in the liberation of eternal spirit from transient matter. This means depersonalization in order to be merged in the absolute, or to realize oneself as the absolute, or as an independent spiritual monad, or as 'part' of the absolute, identical with it in respect of being but separate from it insofar as it is the source of becoming.

(b) Buddhism: man is simply a bundle of sensations, intellections, etc. There is no such thing as an individual self that holds together and co-ordinates anything that can be called personality. 'Salvation' is the extinction of desire and therefore of all becoming and development: it is to pass beyond birth and death into a timeless state of being. Both the Hindu and Buddhist views of 'salvation' are conditioned by their belief in the transmigration of souls. Because life is an endless repetition of more or less miserable existences, there can be no 'salvation' without the extinction of life as we know it.

(c) Judaism: man is created 'in the image of God' from the dust of the earth: he is brought to life by the spirit or 'breath' of God. Destined to be immortal, he sins and thereby forfeits his immortality. He is a unitary being, and death of the individual is therefore total. There can thus be no salvation of the individual as distinct from the totality of the race. Salvation must therefore be seen as taking place in the future when the kingdom of God, of justice and peace, will be established on earth.

(d) Zoroastrianism: man and the whole material world are created by the good God, Ohrmazd, as a defence against his *spiritual* antagonist, Ahriman. His soul survives bodily death, is judged and receives his reward or punishment in accordance with his good or evil deeds. In the last days all souls are purged in molten metal, receive back their bodies and enjoy eternal bliss with God in a new heaven and a new earth. The devil is destroyed or forever made inoperative.

(e) Islam: man, like everything else, is willed into existence by God's creative word. He is judged both according to his faith and

infidelity and in accordance with his good and evil deeds though, according to orthodox doctrine, these are eternally predestined by God. The good are rewarded in paradise where they will see God, the wicked are condemned to the fire forever.

4. What is the relationship of man to God?

In Buddhism the question does not arise. In Islam the relationship is that of slave to master: only in Sūfīsm does an element of love appear. In Judaism man is God's servant, but Israel, the chosen people, is bound to him by an eternal covenant. She is also his wayward spouse, but despite her infidelities, she will return to him and be the instrument of the salvation of all mankind.

In Hinduism man is not truly an individual, and his final bliss is to realize this and to merge into the All which is at the same time the One. This is the usual Upanishadic view. Only when God and man come to be regarded as distinct can we properly speak of relationships. Then the proper relationship of man to God is *bhakti* – loyalty, devotion, and love. This idea first becomes prominent in the Bhagavad-Gītā in which the God Krishna rules both our world of time and space and the 'other' timeless world. Hence true *bhakti* survives man's liberation from the material world and takes on an eternal dimension. As the Gītā (18.54-5) says: 'Once he has become Brahman, with self serene, he neither grieves nor desires; the same to all contingent beings he gains the highest love and loyalty to me. By love and loyalty he comes to know me as I really am, how great I am and who; and once he knows me as I am, he enters me forthwith.'

Now, from this very brief analysis of the cardinal doctrines of the principal faiths it is clear that there is very little in common between the Semitic group and the Indian one. Religion, however, does not stand still. Like everything else it is an evolutionary process; and it is only now when we have come to know so much more about non-Christian religions, that we can begin to discern a pattern in their very discrepancies and conflicts. If by 'truth' we mean something that corresponds to the deepest instincts of mankind, we can say that the religions themselves discard what no longer appears to be relevant to them and retain what seems permanently relevant and true. Hinduism is the classic example of this: the Vedic Saṁhitās and Brāhmaṇas plus a lot of early Upanishadic material are quietly consigned to the lumber-room, and the Bhagavad-Gītā comes to assume enormous importance. In Islam the Sūfīs did much the same with the Qur'ān and Traditions: they were silent about what seemed to them incompatible with their own experience of a living and loving God and embraced (or invented) doubtful traditions often not accepted as authentic by the orthodox.

Alternatively, one religion borrows from another and absorbs so much 'truth' into itself that the religion from which it borrows finally disappears. This was the fate of Zoroastrianism, whose leading prophetic insights were absorbed into post-exilic Judaism and thence into Christianity and Islam. Before the exile Yahweh was, as Jung has pointed out, a wildly disconcerting amalgam of God and the devil; and had it not been for Israel's contact with Iran, Jesus could scarcely have said: 'Why do you call me good? No one is good but God alone,'[21] nor could the devil have developed from the comparatively innocuous status he occupies in the Old Testament into the formidable adversary of God and man we meet with in the Gospel and Epistles of St John. His role is somewhat attenuated in the Qur'ān but the Qur'ānic doctrine of an eternal heaven and hell is not only faithful to its Zoroastrian prototype that it inherited via Christianity but greatly surpasses the original. The 'truth' that Zoroastrianism enunciated was that evil is so monstrous a thing that it would be sheer blasphemy to attribute it to God. But once it was elevated to the rank of a separate cosmic principle it collided with another 'truth' which is affirmed in most other religions whether Semitic or Indian, namely, that there is only one God – one absolute, if you like – manifesting himself in the phenomenal world. And so Christianity and Islam absorbed the concept of the devil, but did not allow him the status of a separate principle, thus preserving the unity of God.

On the Hindu side the Bhagavad-Gītā inaugurates what is in fact a new religion, built on the insights of both the Upanishads and Buddhism, but adding and affirming the existence and primacy of a personal and incarnate God who transcends both time and eternity. Similarly Jesus, particularly in the writings of Paul and John – inaugurates a new covenant – a new religion which, from the very beginning, had to separate itself from Judaism because it was affirmed of Jesus that not only was he the Messiah but also the Son of God and God himself. In India the *bhakti* cults inaugurated by the Bhagavad-Gītā were to become the dominant religion of the people; so too did Christianity slowly become the religion of the

Roman Empire while Judaism, renouncing its potential universal-
ism, now turned in upon itself, remaining a purely national religion.
Both the Gītā and Christianity are bridges between Semitic transcendentalism and Indian immanentism. In Christianity the 'wholly
other' becomes Emmanuel, the God in us and among us, while in
the Gītā (14.27) the immanent God of the Upanishads emerges as
the utterly transcendent – 'the base supporting Brahman – immortal Brahman which knows no change – supporting too the
eternal law of righteousness and absolute beatitude'.

The incarnation is, of course, central to Christianity. It is, as
St Paul says, an insurmountable obstacle to the Jews (and, of course,
to the Muslims too) and pure madness to the pagans, that is, to
rational philosophy. Yet it is a doctrine that struck firm roots in
Hinduism, and it appears in the shape of the *nirmāṇa-kāya* in
Mahāyāna Buddhism, and Muhammad himself is deified by Al-
Ḥallāj and the Sūfīs who follow him. This, then, seems to be another,
though less general a 'truth', that is liable to turn up in all religions;
but only in Christianity is it crucial.

In Christianity, Christ, who is sinless, is 'begotten' of God, and
through him all Christians who 'die' with Christ in the waters of
baptism[22], are themselves 'begotten of God' and therefore sinless[23]:
in other words they participate fully in Christ's divinity. And this is
precisely what we find in Mahāyāna Buddhism, particularly in the
Lotus Sūtra. The final aim is not Nirvāṇa, which corresponds to
baptismal death, but the discovery of the Buddha-nature within
one – eternal wisdom and unfailing compassion. Thus in Christianity, developed Hinduism, and Mahāyāna Buddhism we have the
same mystical descent of God and ascent of man: God becomes
man in order that man may become God. In Hindu terms the
Christian mystery can be explained in this way. Christ, like Krishna,
is for all time *brahma-bhūta*: before his incarnation he is a pure
ātman – or rather the pure *Ātman* – God in every sense of the word.
He, however, descends into matter and becomes as other men are.
He dies on the cross; but, according to the Gītā, it is not only the
ego that must die, the *ātman* can die too (16.21). It is shaken out
of its timelessness at the vision of God seen as the avenger and
destroyer (11.24). So too Christ must undergo the agony of the
cross before he can transcend eternity itself and be re-united with
his seemingly 'terrible' Father. The Buddha too endures the agony
of near-despair when he realizes that the way of extreme asceticism
brings him no nearer to Nirvāṇa. Nirvāṇa, however, according to

the Mahāyāna, is not the end but simply *requies aeterna*, final death
beyond the recurrent births and deaths in *saṁsāra*. His *parinirvāṇa*
is, however, at the same time a resurrection, for, as with the risen
Christ, out of it proceeds the Dharma, the eternally valid way of
salvation, the Way and the Truth, if not the Life.

What both Hinduism and Buddhism in their different ways teach
us is that the deepest essence of man is beyond space and time, and
this is common to the nature mystics too; but the Gītā and the
Lotus Sūtra go on beyond this and say that the realization of this
brahma-nirvāṇa must be supplemented by union with God or
identification with the Buddha not only as to his eternal being but
also in his transcendent compassion and love. This dual aspect of
the mystical experience can be seen in all the mystical traditions;
but in India it is the identity of being that comes first; the identity in
difference that is the essence of both temporal and eternal love
comes later. The danger is that a man will get stuck in Nirvāṇa,
thinking that this is the end. In Christian terminology this would
be to remain forever static in the prayer of quiet, which is the
Hīnayāna Nirvāṇa and the *brāhmī sthitiḥ* of the Gītā. This is
dangerous both for the individual and for any religious community
that makes Nirvāṇa its sole end. Indeed there is much wisdom in
the aphorism of Aurobindo we are about to quote, for it enables
us to see the relevance of Islam in the concordant discord of faiths
that, may one say, result in a final harmony: 'Muhammad's mission
was necessary, else we might have ended by thinking, in the exaggeration of our efforts at self-purification, that earth was meant
only for the monk and the city created as a vestibule for the
desert'.[24]

True enough, for it was, after all, Islam that dealt the final death-
blow to Buddhism in India, as it had done to the ascetic Christianity
of North Africa and Syria. The moral of this would seem to be that
no religion can hope to evoke what La Rochefoucauld calls the
'truth' (*le vrai*) in all of us, if it writes off this world entirely, any
more than it can succeed if it turns its back entirely on the contemplation of the divine. Whether or not Islam's essential triumph-
alism is, from the religious point of view, justified, must remain a
moot question; but had its conquest of the world for the faith not
been counterbalanced by the contemplative quest of the Sūfīs, it is
doubtful whether it could have maintained its position, let alone
expanded it by peaceful means as it has done in Indonesia and
Africa. So too the strength of the Catholic Church has been not in

its hierarchical structure, but in the fact that its central rites, baptism and the eucharist, are essentially mystical since, for the individual, they represent the death of the ego and the birth of the immortal 'self' and the union of the latter with the Man-God Christ present both spiritually and materially in the eucharist. So too the Church, as a human collectivity, sees itself as the *material* body of Christ here on earth, as a prolongation and an extension of the incarnation itself. In it both Mary and Martha have their allotted parts.

In the *Kaṭha* Upanishad (4.1) we read:

The self-existent [Lord] bored holes facing the outside world;
Therefore a man looks outward, not into himself.
A certain sage, in search of immortality,
Turned his eyes inward and saw the self within.

Both Hinduism and Buddhism have come to realize that the 'inwardness' that has for so long characterized them both, has gone too far: hence the Hindu reformers, and particularly Gandhi, Tagore, and Aurobindo, have striven to redress the balance: they have turned their eyes outward to see the world without. The same process of adjustment may be seen in Japanese Buddhism; for although Zen is still making progress in the West and is seen by some as a means by which the inner life of the Christian Church might be revitalized, there is some evidence that it is losing ground in Japan itself. The really significant development in Japanese religion is not Zen but the emergence of Neo-Nichirenism in the form of Sōka Gakkai with an estimated membership of nearly twenty millions due, one must suppose, to its communal activity and political and social commitment.

To sum up: 'prophetic' religion addresses itself to the community, it is not primarily interested in individuals: 'mystical' religion is of its very nature a matter of individual experience of the eternal, it cannot extend itself to the community. The only religion that has from the beginning been both communal and individual is Christianity: its dual purpose is to build up the body of Christ on earth and to seek out the kingdom of God within you. Hinduism, Buddhism, and Taoism were one-sided in their ultimate rejection of the world, and their activities in the world have never been, until modern times, co-ordinated with their essentially other-worldy ideal. Thus Hinduism preaches oneness of spirit, but has the most divisive social system ever invented by the mind of man. Buddhism has its Saṅgha, of course, which is its physical centre, but this is in no way comparable to the Christian Church or the Muslim *umma* since it corresponds to the monastic orders in Christendom, not to the Church in its entirety. The importance of the community living with a common spiritual life was realized by Jōsei Toda in Japan, and the immense success of Sōka Gakkai of which he was the charismatic inspiration, proves that no religion can continue as a vital force if it is not of immediate revelance to the community. The drive towards the integration of these two aspects of religion, the personal and the collective, has been characteristic of the most original thinkers in the field of religion during the first two-thirds of the twentieth century. In Islam we have Iqbal, in Hinduism Aurobindo, in Christianity Teilhard de Chardin, in Buddhism Makiguchi and Toda. All are striving towards the realization of the catholic idea (which is also the authentic doctrine of the Catholic Church), and which in Hinduism was long ago proclaimed on a cosmic scale in the Bhagavad-Gītā: for what was revealed to Arjuna in Krishna's stupendous theophany was the coherence of all things in the divine centre – the transfigured body of the lord, whether you call the lord Krishna, Christ, or Buddha: 'Then did the son of Pāṇḍu see the whole universe in One converged, there in the body of the God of gods, yet divided out in multiplicity' (Gītā, 11.13). This is the meaning of the Church as the body of Christ, and this is the goal to which evolution itself is pointing. This unity in diversity is the birthright of the Catholic Church: and I hope it is not presumptuous to say that just as all Christians are 'other Christs' insofar as they are 'begotten of God', so do all the other religions, in their historical development, grow into 'other Catholic Churches', each converging onto its own Omega point, as Teilhard de Chardin puts it, its own Mahdi, Maitreya, or Kalkin; for the name and the object of each particularist worship does not matter so very much. The enemy of all of us is satan, the principle of division, dissociation, and discord *der Geist der stets verneint*, but the spirit that works in secret, building us all into a 'spiritual house'[25], is the Holy Spirit, the God who is the inspiration of all religions and peculiar to none, *der Geist der stets verneint*.

NOTES

1 John 18.37-8.
2 Mark 14.61-4.
3 E. T. Sachau, *Al-Beruni's India* (London, 1888), vol 1, p. 19.
4 *Chāndogya* Upanishad, 6.12 2-3.
5 Prov. 1.7.
6 Pierre Teilhard de Chardin, *Oeuvres* 5, p. 101.
7 C. G. Jung, *Answer to Job* (London, Routledge and Kegan Paul, 1954) p. 4.
8 Ibid., p. 3.
9 Sri Aurobindo, *Thoughts and Aphorisms* (Pondicherry, 1958) p. 82.
10 *Śvetāśvatara* Upanishad 6.13.
11 Udāna, p. 80.
12 Qur'ān, 112.
13 Ibid., 57.3.
14 Exod. 3.14.
15 Atharva Veda, 10.2.32 : 10.8.43.
16 Ibid., 10.8.44.
17 *Brihadāraṇyaka* Upanishad, 4.4. 22-3.
18 Jer. 1.10.
19 1 Cor. 1.23.
20 Alan Watts, *Beyond Theology* (London, Hodder & Stoughton, 1964), p. 85.
21 Mark 10.18; Luke 18.19.
22 Rom. 6.4.
23 1 John 3.9.
24 Aurobindo, *Thoughts and Aphorisms*, p. 28.
25 1 Pet. 2.5.

R. C. ZAEHNER is a Fellow of All Souls College and Spalding Professor of Eastern Religions in the University of Oxford. Author of *Hinduism, Mysticism Sacred and Profane*; *At Sundry Times*; *The Teachings of the Magi*; *The Dawn and Twilight of Zoroastrianism*; *The Convergent Spirit*; *The Bhagavad Gītā*; *Evolution in Religion*; *Dialectial Christianity and Christian Materialism*; *Drugs, Mysticism and Make-Believe*, etc.

A Human View of Truth

WILFRED CANTWELL SMITH

In this paper I wish to present a position on the notion 'truth', to develop it, and to argue on its behalf.

Let me begin with a statement of the thesis in highly summary form. Briefly, my suggestion is that the locus of truth is persons. Or, if not 'the' locus, at least a central locus: one of considerably greater importance and primacy than are usually nowadays recognized. Truth and falsity are often felt in modern times to be properties or functions of statements or propositions; whereas the present proposal is that much is to be gained by seeing them rather, or anyway by seeing them also, and primarily, as properties or functions of persons.

In a nutshell, then, this presents the position that I must now try to develop. In order to elucidate it, my plan is to turn to Islamic civilization, and to draw from it my illustrative material. I do so partly because that is the sector of human affairs that I have studied most closely. I do it also, in part, because I hold – I have found – that in principle there is illumination, and potential profit, in considering any human problem thus from an unwonted angle, and in a wider context; pondering how a matter has appeared to men in other civilizations, and comparing that with how it appears to us. A comparativist approach to almost any issue can prove not only refreshing but instructive: our civilization is no longer faring so gratifyingly that we can blandly ignore criteria that transcend it. Thirdly, this approach illustrates my thesis not only substantially but formally: it is part of my contention that academic study, in so far as it is a pursuit of truth, involves also a question as to its truth for us, a question such as I here raise. Chiefly, however, I present this Islamic material because it seems to me saliently helpful: to illustrate with clarity and force a matter of significance for us all.

Naturally, I have no wish to involve those unfamiliar with Islamics in exotic technicalities any more than necessary. We shall be able, however, I believe, to make my point clear by calling attention simply to three roots in the Arabic language, around which crystallized Muslims' concepts on this central issue. These three will, I think, suffice to illumine for us the Islamic stance, and to set the stage for our consideration not only of their orientations but also then of our own.

The three Arabic terms are *ḥaqqa, ṣadaqa,* and *saḥḥa.* All three have something to do with truth. Yet the three are quite distinct (and this fact in itself can serve us instructively). If I might over-simplify in order to introduce my point, I would suggest that the first has to do with the truth of things, the second with the truth of persons, and the third with the truth of statements. But let me elaborate.

First, *ḥaqqa.*

When I first learned Arabic, I was taught that *ḥaqq* sometimes means 'true', sometimes means 'real'. Now this same remark, actually, had been made also about the Latin term *verus,* which can mean real, genuine, authentic, and also true, valid. When I came to learn Sanskrit, I met the same point again with regard to that language (and civilization's) term *satyam*: it too denotes both reality, and truth. Eventually I came to realize that what was happening here was not necessarily that all these peoples were somehow odd folk who had confused or converged two concepts, or used one word indiscriminately for two different notions; but rather that it is perhaps we who are odd, or off the track, we who have somehow dichotomized a single truth-reality, and have allowed our conception of truth to diverge from our conception of reality. At least, a strong case can be made for such a view.

Even in the West today we harbour remnants of this earlier usage. For our own civilization, decidedly, was built upon concepts of this type. We still at times can speak of true courage, or false modesty; of true marriage or a true university; even of a true note in music. I mentioned this once, however, to a philosopher only to have him dismiss it as metaphorical, and not really legitimate or even significant. Only propositions, he said, are *really* true or false. And even for non-analysts among us, whatever our residual vocabulary, there has come to be widespread today a certain discomfort, most will probably agree, with any but a very imprecise position that things, qualities, actions, can be true or false. Things are just there, somehow, many feel, and it is only what we say about them that is subject to this discriminating judgement.

However that may be, in Arabic *ḥaqq* like *satyam* and *veritas* refers to what is real, genuine, authentic, what is true in and of itself by dint of metaphysical or cosmic status. It is a term par excellence of God. In fact, it refers absolutely to him, and indeed *al-Ḥaqq* is a name of God not merely in the sense of an attribute but of a denotation. *Huwa al-Ḥaqq* : He is a reality as such. Yet every other thing that is genuine is also *ḥaqq* – and some of the mystics went on to say, is therefore divine. Yet the word means reality first, and then God, for those who equate him with reality. It is somewhat interesting, in passing, that this in a sense makes it more engaging (perhaps more realistic?) to talk about atheism in Arabic than in English, since in Arabic the question can become whether one believes in Reality, whether one trusts Reality, whether one commits oneself to Reality, and the like. Yet I let that pass. We simply note that *ḥaqq* is truth in the sense of the real, with or without a capital R.

Secondly, let us turn to the Arabic *ṣadaqa*. As I have remarked, this term refers to a truth of persons. It matches to some extent our Western notions of honesty, integrity, and trustworthiness: yet it goes beyond them. It involves being true both to oneself and to other persons, and to the situation with which one is dealing. Propositional truth is by no means irrelevant here. It is not ruled out; nor even set aside. Rather, it is subordinated, being incorporated as an element within a personalist context. For indeed the term is used predominantly, although not exclusively, for what we call 'telling the truth'. This is often the simplest way to translate it; yet there is something more. What that something more involves, at the personalist level, becomes apparent when we consider, in both Arabic and English, the contrasting concept of telling a lie. *Ṣadaqa* is the precise opposite of *kadhiba*, 'to be a liar'. This latter, as is its translation with us, is a highly revealing usage. For it denotes the saying of something that not only is untrue, but that also the speaker knows to be untrue and says with an intent to deceive. The Arabs normally do not use *kadhiba*, as we do not use 'liar', in the case where a man says something inaccurate but in good faith.

It is curious, as we shall develop later, that in English we have the concept 'lie' and 'liar', which corresponds more or less exactly to the Islamic concept of *kadhiba*, a personal falsity, untruth at the level of human intent and practice, and of interpersonal relations, but we do not have an exact equivalent to, have not formulated a special concept for, the counterpart notion of *ṣidq* : truth of the strictly personalist focus. (*Ṣidq* is the generic of *ṣadaqa* : what modern Westerners call the abstract noun, although for Arabs it is more strictly the verbal noun, the name of the action.)

This concept, then, has been a central one for Muslims, not least in their religious life, and is central too for the thesis that I am endeavouring to advance in this paper. I will turn to pursue it further, therefore, presently. We set it aside for a moment to deal with the third term, *ṣaḥḥa*.

This verb, and its adjective *ṣaḥīḥ*, although expressing important notions, have been less spectacular in Islamic life, and especially in the realm that concerns us here. The words mean, more or less, 'sound', and refer to quite a variety of matters, such as being healthy or being appropriate. One would hardly think of it right off as a term for 'truth' at all, except that its usage does, indeed, overlap in part with that of that English word in that it may be used in Arabic of propositions when they are what we would call true or correct (*hādhā ṣaḥīḥ, hādhā ghalaṭ* – or, *khāṭiʾ*; or simply *ghayr ṣaḥīḥ*).

Of these three Arabic concepts, it is to be noted that the first two have strongly polarized contraries. *Ḥaqq* stands in stark and even awesome contrast to *bāṭil*, as the true and the false, or the real and the 'phoney'. Behind the one is metaphysical power, while the other in strident dichotomy from it is ludicrously vain and vacuous. To distinguish between the two is one of man's most decisive tasks or prerogatives. Again, there is the resonant pair of *ṣidq* and *kādhib*, or, to use the more concrete human terms, *ṣādiq* and *kādhib*: the honest man of truth stands sharply over against the despicable and wretched liar. At play here is the Islamic vision of man's dramatic freedom and moral choice, in a world where decisions matter.

Ṣaḥīḥ, on the other hand, has no clear opposite. One of its applications is to a man's being in sound health; possible alternatives are that he may be weak, or sick, or old, or not old enough, or missing a limb, or whatnot; but there is no clear other pole. The only opposite of 'sound' is a wide range of unsoundness, of unspecified imperfections; although as we have already noted, in the particular case of a sentence, if it is not *ṣaḥīḥ*, true, then one may perhaps call it mistaken, *ghalaṭ* or *khāṭiʾ*. A railway timetable that is no longer in force, or an argument that is not cogent, various sorts of things that do not come off or are not in good working order, may be characterized as not *ṣaḥīḥ*; but this designates a quality that is not a category, or at least not a cosmic one. In other Islamic languages too – Persian, Urdu, and others, as well as Arabic, those familiar with these languages will readily agree – this third notion, used for, among other things, propositional truth, has by far the feeblest moral connotations of the three.[1]

Indeed, the first and the second are saturatedly, bristlingly, moral; they, and their respective pejorative contraries, are highly moralistic. Human destiny is at stake with them, and human quality. And, appropriately enough, it turns out on inquiry that the third root, *ṣaḥḥa*, does not even occur in the Qur'ān. The other two reverberate in it, mightily.

It would hardly be an exaggeration to see the Qur'ān as a vibrant affirmation that the *loci* of significant truth are two: the world around us, and persons. The reality of the former is divine, or is God. The inner integrity of the latter, and our conformity to, and commitment to, the real, are crucial. Indeed, this is what human life is all about.[2]

Let us return, however, to our specifically linguistic item: *ṣadaqa*, *ṣidq*. Being a resonant term in the Qur'ān, it formulates for Muslims a cosmic category, constituting one of the basic points of reference in relation to which human life and society take on meaning in the Islamic complex. Even apart from the rest of that complex, however, I think that we may find it a strikingly interesting conceptualization in itself, one that will reward a rather careful unfolding.

First, let us look at the great medieval Arabic dictionaries, those marvellous mines of massive yet meticulous information. We find in them illuminating presentations and analyses of this word. Almost always these are given in conjunction with its correlative, *kadhiba*, 'lying'. The dictionary expositions in almost every case give first, or make quite basic, the link with speech. Yet even so it is (it and 'lying' are) applied to all sorts of things that man may say (and not only to what in modern logic would be called statements or propositions). Explicitly indicated is that the speech may be about the past or about the future, in the latter case whether by way of promise or otherwise; and may be indicative but also either interrogative or imperative, and even supplicative. Thus a question may be not *ṣidq*, truthful, if it involves something of the 'Have you stopped beating your wife?' sort. Similarly a command, such as 'Give me back my book', or an entreaty, 'Would you please give me back my book', may be *ṣidq* or *kadhib*, truthful or lying, depending upon whether the man addressed has the book, and the person speaking genuinely wishes it back.

In general, the dictionaries make it clear that the point is that *ṣidq* applies to that sort of speech in which there is conformity of what is said simultaneously with two things: (a) what is in the speaker's mind; and (b) what is actually the case.

Particular discussion is given to an assertion that 'Muḥammad is the Apostle of God' – which is the Muslim's paradigm of a true statement – when it is made by someone who says it insincerely. One view is that any utterance may be half *ṣidq*, in reference either to the speaker's sincerity or to the objective facts, but there is full *ṣidq* only when both are satisfied. Similarly, when there is reference to the future, then *ṣidq* demands congruity both between inner conviction and a man's words and between the latter and his subsequent deeds.

The verb may take a direct object of the person addressed, inasmuch as telling the truth, in this sense, and lying, are matters of personal interrelations. 'He lied to him', or 'P spoke the truth to Q', indicate that the truth and falsity under consideration here are attributes of a statement in its role of establishing or constituting communication between or among human beings. Here again, it may be noted that in the modern West we maintain in our conceptualization of lying the notion that one can hardly tell a lie alone on a desert island, but we have tended to let go this interpersonal dimension from our conception of speaking truth.

Comparable considerations operate when the Arabic verb is used of human actions other than speaking. Transitional is a phase such as *ṣadaqahu al-naṣīḥah*: 'He was true in the advice that he gave him', or 'He spoke the truth to him in his advice', or 'He advised him with *ṣidq*'. This implies that the counsel was both sincere, and effectively wise. Non-verbally: *Ṣadaqahu al-ikhā'*, 'He was true towards him in brotherliness', or '... behaved towards him with true brotherhood'. Again: *ṣadaqūhum al-gitāl*, 'They fought them with *ṣidq*', 'They were true against them in battle'. This means that they fought against them both with genuine zeal and with good effect.

Throughout, *ṣidq* is that quality by which a man speaks or acts with a combination of inner integrity and objective overt appropriateness. It involves saying or doing the objectively right thing out of a genuine personal recognition of its rightness, an inner alignment with it.

In modern English we have negative concepts such as lying and cheating, which conceptualize overt performance in terms of the performers and their moral quality as well as in terms of the objective outward facts or rules. On the other hand, we have not developed carefully, or formulated strongly, counterpart positive concepts to assess and to interpret behaviour in these trilateral[3] terms. This is what the notion *ṣadaqa* precisely does.

Human behaviour, in word or deed, is the nexus between man's inner life and the surrounding world. Truth at the personalist level is that quality by which both halves of that relationship are chaste and appropriate; are true.

The Muslims were no fools when they regarded this as an important human category.

There remains yet one more move. For man's relation to the truth, though intimate and integral, is not simply passive. Our next step is to follow the Arabs, an activist people, into a further development of this same term, one that activates the concept and renders it transitive. For man not only holds the truth in his heart, but also acts it out.

In Arabic, as in other Semitic languages (as those who may know Hebrew will recognize), there is a formal pattern whereby by manipulating the consonants of a root, and specifically by doubling the middle letter, a given notion is intensified, in various complicated ways, and especially is made causative.

Thus in the case at which we have been looking, from *ṣadaqa*, 'To speak the truth, to act truly, to be true', is formed *ṣaddaqa*, the so-called *tafʿīl* form: basically, 'To make come true', 'to render true'. It is an intricate causative or double transitive of wide potentiality. The verbal noun in this case is *taṣdīq*, the act or generic quality designated by this verb *ṣaddaqa*.

Let us look at it for a moment.

The simple form (*ṣadaqa*) means to say (or to do) something that is at the same time both inwardly honest and outwardly correct. What then does the reactivated form (*taṣdīq*) signify? I will list four meanings.

First: it can mean 'to regard as true'. Its primary object may be either a person, or a sentence; so that *ṣaddaqahu*, or he gave him or it *taṣdīq*, may mean 'he held him to be a speaker of the truth', or 'he held it to be spoken truly'. These can be rendered, if you like, as 'he believed him' (or: 'it'): but in both cases, because he trusted the speaker. It can indicate that he held him to be *ṣādiq*, a speaker sincerely of truth on a particular occasion, or held him to be *ṣiddīq*, an habitual teller of the truth by moral character. A rendition by 'believe' is, moreover, inadequate also because it omits the reference to objective validity, since 'believe' in English has become so openly neutral a term. One can believe what is false. I have not checked enough passages to be able to affirm flatly that *taṣdīq* applies only to believing what is in fact true, and yet I think that there can be no question but that, even if there are some exceptions, the standard implication still is strongly one of objective truth as well as of sincerity. This is a cosmic human quality, with little room for sheer gullibility. Accordingly, one should translate, at this level, not by 'believe' but by 'recognize the truth of'. The difference is crucial.

Even this, however, takes care of only one side of the double reference, that to the correctness of what is so regarded. There is still the other side, the personal sincerity involved. This operates at least as strongly in this second form as in the first. And the personalism is of both the primary subject and the secondary: to recognize a truth as personal for others, and as personal for oneself. Thus, if I give *taṣdīq* to some statement, I not merely recognize its truth in the world outside me, and subscribe to it, but also incorporate it into my own moral integrity as a person.

A second standard usage of this form is that it means, not 'he held him to be a speaker of the truth', but rather 'he *found* him to be' so. One may hear a man's statement, and only subsequently find reason or experience to know that that man was no liar.

Thirdly, it may indicate this sort of notion but with a more active, resolute type of finding: that is, 'he *proved* him to be a speaker of truth', or confirmed or verified the matter. Thus there is a common phrase (*ṣaddaqa al-khabara al-khubru*): 'The experience verified the report'. Accordingly, *taṣdīq* has become the term for scientific experimental verification, proving something true by test; although the notion of vindicating the experimenter as well as the experiment is never far distant. A stricter translation of the phrase just quoted would be 'the experiment verified the report and the reporter'.

Fourthly, still more deliberately, *taṣdīq* may mean to render true, to take steps to make come true. One instance of this is one's own promise: a radically important matter. Or it may apply to another's promise. Or, to another's remark. If you say that that window will be closed, and I go and close it, then I have given *taṣdīq* to you. (Recently, I came across a passage in the most fundamental of Muslim commentaries on the Qur'ān, that of al-Ṭabarī, where he uses the two forms of the verb in a single revealing sentence. He refers to a group of people who spoke the truth with their tongues, but did not go on to give to what they had said *taṣdīq* in their deeds[4]. We could translate here: 'They did not corroborate – or, authenticate – their speech by their deeds'.)

To summarize. *Taṣdīq* is to recognize a truth, to appropriate it, to affirm it, to confirm it, to actualize it, And the truth, in each case, is personalist and sincere.

All of this is in general: this work has been done primarily on the basis of the medieval Arabic dictionaries. I turn now to specifically theological interpretations. For classical Muslim thinkers, when asked what faith is, affirmed almost to a man that it is *taṣdīq*. As an historian of religion, I have been particularly interested in various conceptions of faith around the world, and this one not least. If we ponder this formula a little, and correlate it with the several versions that we have just noted of *taṣdīq*, we can see that it makes good sense, and can see what the men of religion meant when they said that faith is doing or making or activating truth: doing personal truth, or making truth personal.

To begin with, faith is then the *recognition* of divine truth at the personal level. Faith is the ability to recognize truth as true for oneself – and to trust it. Especially in the Islamic case, with its primarily moral orientation, this includes, or makes primary, the recognition of the authenticity and moral authority of the divine commands. Thus there is the recognition of the obligatoriness of moral obligations; and the acceptance of their obligatoriness as applying to oneself, with the personal commitment then to carrying them out.

Again, it is the personal making of what is cosmically true come true on earth: the *actualization* of truth (the truth about man).

More mystically, it is the *discovery* of the truth (the personal truth) of the Islamic injunctions: the process of personal verification of them, whereby by living them out one proves them and finds that they do indeed become true, both for oneself and for the society and world in which one lives.

Taṣdīq is the inner appropriation and outward implementation of truth: the process of making or finding true in actual human life, in one's own personal spirit and overt behaviour, what God – or reality – intends for man.

And, with many a passage strongly insisting that faith is more than knowledge, that it is a question of how one responds to the truth, one may also render the proposition 'faith is *taṣdīq*' as 'Faith is the ability to trust, and to act in terms of, what one knows to be true'.

All these are not bad definitions of faith, one will perhaps agree. They are not, and are not meant to be, definitions of Islamic faith; rather, they are Islamic definitions of human faith. At issue here is not the content of faith but its form; not its object but its nature. In question is not what is true, but what one does about what is true[5].

Let me conclude, then, this part of my presentation by summing up the Islamic vision of *ṣidq*, in its fundamentally moral and human terms. Truth, as a relation to the world, is seen as existing also in relation to man; and man is seen as acting in relation to truth.

For the final section of my talk, I would like us to consider these matters in relation to modern Western society.

The transition from the one to the other may itself need clarification. First; there is the both logical and moral point that this orientation, at which we have been looking as it were from a distance, itself requires that that distance, that non-*engagé* objectivity and neutralist observationism, be replaced with an existential concern, a wrestling with the implications for oneself. The very suggestion that truth is not an inert and impersonal observable but that truth means truth for me, for you, is challenging. Let us face the challenge.

Secondly, more traditionally in our society, and professionally, of course, it has been the task of philosophers to deal with the concept of truth; and I am not a philosopher. I am, rather, an historian. My not being a philosopher explains many disabilities, which will be sorely conspicuous in a gathering of this sort. Yet being a cultural historian is perhaps not so irrelevant as it might at first seem. At least, it explains my concern. The study of history, too, may contribute something to understanding in this realm. And vice versa: the question of truth has enormous significance for history. How truth is conceived, where it is looked for, are historical issues as well as theoretical. A comparative study of human history around the globe recognizes that different civilizations and ages have had differing visions of truth; and it must report that the choice can manifestly be of decisive consequence.

It is the cultural historian who sees how terribly important these questions can be, in the development or the disintegration of a society. The cultural historian may also see the technical philosophy of any civilization as in some fashion within the particular development of that civilization at a given time; and may ask in the case

of a society that seems, like ours, to be perhaps seriously ill, whether
the ideas with which it is operating may conceivably be boundaried
within the illness. The 'ordinary language' of a society may illustrate
the limitations as well as the insights of that age and that particular
culture.

In any case, I am bold enough to ask whether the recent loss of
a sense of the personal quality of truth may not be a serious illness.
One may wonder whether the Western surrender of what seem,
from a larger world perspective, to be important ingredients in
human life and its awareness of reality, may not have contributed
significantly to our malaise.

The concept of the truth of things I leave aside; not because it
seems unimportant, but simply for lack of time. The purpose of this
present paper is to champion the personalist level of truth, so that
it would be distracting to complicate the argument by advocating a
certain worthiness also (still?) in the realist (or if one prefers,
idealist) level – although personally I am persuaded that the observations of a cultural historian in analysing what has happened
to our society as a result of losing this apprehension of transcendence could be startling.

So far as personalist truth is concerned, on which I will con-
centrate, it seems to me clear that monumental consequences have
followed on our letting go of our hold on this dimension, and the
resultant divorce between truth and morality. (The other loss
signified a divorce in our awareness between reality and morality.)
Modern Western thinkers are aware that earlier ages saw things
differently, or at least spoke of things differently; but they tend to
leave aside social consequences, and to believe on purely theoretical
grounds that the divorces have constituted an advance in clarity. I
am less interested in clarity than in truth and goodness; and I have
a suspicion that the world is in fact more complicated, especially
in its interconnections and in man's relations to it, than modern
theories sometimes know.

Not that we have lost this apprehension totally. As with the
truth of things, so also here for personalist truths the modern
Western world does preserve remnants of an older orientation, in a
few of its phrases. We speak of a man's being true to his word, of
course, but also true to his wife, or true to his office. Or we may
say that given his responsibilities, he acted falsely. And apparently
the word 'true' is originally cognate with 'trust' (and 'troth').

These kinds of truth and falsity, however, are not much investigated in the modern university.

It is possible to discern a long-range development that has been taking place.

In our Western tradition, greatly to oversimplify, one may perhaps aphorize that the notion of the truth of things is Platonic, that of the truth of propositions Aristotelian. Platonism is no longer strong in our day, of course; although some would add, alas. Aristotle is hardly to be taxed, however, with recent extreme developments of the other tendency, and particularly the current emphasis on specifically impersonal propositions.

This latter emphasis has perhaps not mattered so much in the realm of the natural sciences, where it began; but we shall ask whether it has not become a more serious problem when first social scientists, and then philosophers, have followed. (One realizes that one is taking on quite an array of authorities, then, when one questions the development!) Natural scientists deliberately and with success strive to construct impersonal statements, sentences whose meaning and whose truth are both independent of who makes them. And they see the truth of a statement as in large measure precisely a function of its impersonality. Involved in this has been the rise, and of course the brilliant, indeed spectacular, success, of the objective method, of relentless analysis (as distinct from synthesis), and of all that we know as scientific.

In the study of the natural world, this seems to do not only much good, but concomitantly little harm; although recently both nuclear weapons and ecological problems raise a new issue as to whether even in the natural sciences the amoral, impersonal approach is quite so unchallengeable as one used to think. However that may be, it is not difficult to argue that applying this approach in other areas of inquiry has been imitative at best, disastrous at worst, and one might suggest, perhaps illegitimate throughout. I particularly wish to query the vision that it is legitimate or helpful to regard truth, and falsity, as pertaining to statements considered apart from the person who makes them or about whom they are made. There are some statements, of course, whose truth, and indeed whose meaning, turn, and are meant to turn, on the question of who says them: statements such as 'I am twenty years old', which is false if I make it but true if someone else does. Now it is of course possible to construct special ways of dealing with these so as to avoid, or at least adequately to handle, the problems that are involved. It is also possible, of course, to translate all such statements into more manageable impersonalisms, although I am not sure that this is a healthy impetus. There are some extremely important sentences of this sort, such as 'I love you'.[6]

To elaborate this point, let me turn to another area than propositions altogether, that of games. I should like to reflect upon a game of basketball. First, however, in order to set up an analogy, let me recall the Arabic usage that we considered earlier, when I cited: 'They fought with ṣidq'. Now a counterpart to that idea is preserved in our modern colloquialism. 'That was a real battle!' In the case of games, I find it interesting to reflect on the case of a basketball game that turns out to have been rigged – so that the players were only pretending to compete, while in fact they were deceptively, perhaps with great skill, going through the motions of the contest and actually contriving to achieve a priorly determined (and paid-for) result. Now popularly, such a contest would not be called 'a real game'. In this I find evidence that despite the prevalence of strict positivistic empiricism, and despite an intellectual formulation of that mood philosophically, in fact our society preserves here some remnants of a stand that interprets even the objective world, and assesses its facts, in terms of the moral integrity of the participants. In this instance it is not merely the personal character of the players that is being judged according to moral criteria, but the nature of the observable events. The set of actual (observable) activities in two cases could be identical: yet it would be affirmed that the moral qualities of the actors determined whether what was taking place is in one case 'a game' and in the other case 'not a true game', or even, not a game at all.

Or, putting the point in more linguistic terms, we may say that many of us choose to use the concept 'game' in such a way that it applies only when certain moral factors are operative, and does not apply when these are removed. (Admittedly, one can usually take them for granted.) I hope that the point will not seem blunted by such a shift to language. It is a matter of conceptualization: not simply of how one speaks, but of how one sees and interprets the world, and how one relates oneself to it. The cultural historian might well report that something had been lost in the course of a society's development when that society, let us say in the name of objectivity, has ceased to discriminate, in its language and thought, between a game that is rigged and one that is not.

Similarly as a cultural historian I venture to wonder whether a society has not lost something of major significance once it decides to think of the truth and falsity of statements independently of human and moral involvements. It can be done, of course, as our culture shows. Yet the price one pays is high, as our culture also shows.

Let me not try to persuade, however, so much as to elucidate. In terms of understanding, may we not formulate this equation: that those who can appreciate what is meant by saying that a rigged sports event is not a true game, will be in a position to apprehend what is denoted by the Arabic word *ṣadaqa*[7].

A statement, similarly, might be exactly the same in two cases, but whether that statement is to be called 'true' (*ṣidq*) or not would depend not only on its content but also on the moral intent and involvement with which it is said[8].

Further, I am propounding the suggestion that our society may have historically arrived at a point in its academic and much of its cultural life, with regard to its notion of truth and its activities relating to that notion, where a society would be in its sports life if it had decided that it would use the same concept, and perhaps act in the same way, concerning basketball, regardless of cheating.

That something has gone wrong with our notion of truth is beginning to be suspected also in academia. A question about what sort of thing truth is, has come to haunt, it might seem, the modern university. Student turmoil may be discerned as in part a deep though inchoate restlessness about the particular conception of truth that of late and almost surreptitiously has come to prevail; or perhaps rather, about an inarticulately felt absence of alternative conceptions. In particular, an unreality, and an impersonalism, are sensed, in much of what passes for truth in what the university is engaged in pursuing: a lack of correlation either with absolute significance, with an ultimate, on the one hand, or on the other hand with the inner integrity and wholeness of those persons who are invited to pursue it.

Might we reflect together a little on what kind of transformation might be involved if in a university a personalist conception of truth were to replace the current amoral and impersonal one? Let us take the case of a journal article. For the sake of simplicity we may suppose that it is in some field other than the natural sciences, even though I am not fully sure that we should exclude them. In the social sciences and the humanities, anyway, I feel more confident to speak.

What are we to mean in saying that this article is or is not true?

First, we all agree that such a judgement is concerned with the content of the article, with what it says. Does what it says correspond to the facts, to use traditional phrasing? Is it related to the empirical world in an objective, verifiable way? Is it objectively true, by whatever modern standard for this one chooses?

On this, as I say, all agree: and I discuss it no further. Let me emphasize, however, that this does not mean that I consider it unimportant. I emphasize its significance and indispensability; we move on, simply because it is not controversial. I take it fully for granted.

Many would discuss nothing else. The modern university in general, as well as many modern logicians in particular, are content with this particular dimension of the matter, whatever the pluralism in how it is to be analysed or formulated. The criteria by which this is to be judged, the meaning that it shall have, are questions that we need not settle; we all simply agree that this area of truth is at stake. My suggestion is that there are other additional areas, involving additional criteria and meanings of a quite different sort, that might profitably be brought into play.

For instance: with a personalist concept of truth, the article, no matter what it said, would not be regarded as true if it had been published by someone primarily to get a promotion, or even a reputation.

Thirdly, it could be regarded as not true if it studied human or social affairs without recognizing the personalist level of truth in what was being studied. (This is one of our meanings of *taṣdīq*, one may recall). A researcher who has ferreted out facts and established them (*muḥaqqiq*) or a descriptionist who has made sound (*ṣaḥīḥ*) but impersonal reports about them, as some academics are content to do, would in this orientation be regarded as not having written a *true* article.

In my field of Orientalist studies, there is a type of research practised by remote observers, chiefly Westerners writing only or in principle for a Western audience. In this type of study, the outsider's formulations are never meant to be checked by Asians to see whether the impersonal, so-called objectivist truths are also existentially true, or can become so, in terms of those Asians' personal lives. Similarly in the 'behavioural' sciences, one gets writing whose truth is not calculated for testing by being experimentally subjected to personal verification by those being written about. All writing about human affairs that is formulated only for one's peers in a discipline would come under this stricture.

A counterpart for the social sciences and humanities of the verificationist principle in the natural sciences is the principle that no statement about human affairs is true that cannot be existentially appropriated by those about whom the statement is made.[9]

Finally, no statement might be accepted as true that had not been inwardly appropriated by its author. Studies of that impersonalist kind whose truths make no difference to the moral character of him who deals with them, would be rejected. I have met psychologists who tell me, and without any sheepish embarrassment, that they use determinism as an intellectual hypothesis in their academic work, without necessarily or in fact living their own lives on the determinist principle. For a university or a journal editor to decide not to treat the writing of such men as false, is a major decision.[10]

It might be felt absurdly utopian even to speculate about so radical a transformation of current academic thinking. That is to overlook, I feel, the depth of our present crisis. Human integrity cannot be dismissed as too high a price to pay for reform. Student protest, in all its destructive vehemence, has little vision of a better world and yet is not altogether amiss in its sense that something has gone seriously wrong with the academic world, the intellectual system. It talks of restructuring the university, however, at least in the United States; whereas the significant flaw, I would contend, is not in structures, in organizational patterns, in 'where power lies', and in other such relatively superficial matters. It is rather the ideas dominating and informing our intellectual life that have somehow gone awry – specifically, I am suggesting, the idea that truth can be truly seen as amoral and impersonal.

Those not persuaded of the alternative, personalist position will see two points at issue here: the moral, on the one hand, and the theoretical. In the end, I would argue that the impersonal orientation is intellectually untenable. At a more proximate level, however, one need not suggest that it is logically incoherent. It is far from obviously impossible to construct a total intellectual system, theoretically self-consistent, within which this logic can serve. My thesis is rather, in the first instance, that to choose that system, rather than a more personalist one, is a decision that a society makes, or that we personally make. And it is a fateful decision. To see it so is not simply a personal judgement, but an historical observation. My suggestion is that the system has worked well in the natural sciences (even though that era may be coming to an end), but that it works badly in human affairs.

The history of religion reminds us that total intellectual systems, of great sophistication, power, and elegance, have been constructed for the Islamic, for the medieval Christian, for the monist Hindu, and for other positions; there is no great reason to doubt that comparably consistent systems for amoral propositionalism can be built. History reminds us too that the social and personal consequences of living in accord with any one of those systems have been impressively diverse. It is possible to study, and interesting to discover, what those consequences are.

At this level, then, my thesis is not the logical one that a given system in contemporary Western culture is not self-consistent or even (in the short run) operationally competent. Rather, it is the cultural historian's one that personal and social consequences of mighty proportions are implicit in the orientation that one chooses.

More positively, since the alternative view of truth being propounded inescapably involves morality, one way of formulating the thesis is to say : It is better to see truth as personal. Or perhaps: We ought to see truth thus.

And although I have, on the whole, left aside the natural sciences in my survey, yet it is clear that a serious question is being forcefully pressed about war research and the morality of science in general; even though that question has not been much formulated philosophically, I believe. I am inclined to wonder whether a formulation might not be fruitful in terms of a convergence between personal morality and objective truth.[11]

It is time to close. Yet there remains one phenomenon on our campuses that can be subsumed, I believe, under this same heading. This is the reaction against the establishment, in the name of personalistic 'honesty'. A great to-do has been made in terms of honesty, in ways that seem to me not to solve our society's problem at this level so much as to illustrate it – even perhaps to exacerbate it.

It is intrepid and may seem callous to criticize the notion of honesty these days, since it seems about all that many people have left of their humanity. Yet I think that here too the unification[12] of sincerity and objective rightness is sorely needed. The ideal is personal truth, as I have been contending; but personal truth (*ṣidq*) in an integration in which is involved more than impersonal truth but more also than honesty. For the way to hell is paved with good intentions; just as is the way to Hiroshima or to bacteriological warfare with good objective science.

There is more to the virtue of personalized truth than mere outward propriety or correctness, as I have been arguing all along; yet there is more also than mere sincerity or well-meaning intention. There is no room here for that kind of truth that leaves unaffected the moral character and private behaviour of those who know it. Equally, there is none of that modern nonsense whereby one has simply to unbottle one's emotions, whatever they be, so that feelings are to be expressed regardless of consequences or propriety, or so that we come close to hearing that it is honest to tell a lie provided that one really wants to tell it.

Ṣidq rejects hypocrisy, resoundingly. Yet equally it rejects solipsism and irresponsibility.

If objective truth is not inherently or ideally or conceptually linked with personal life, then personal life is thought of as not to be linked with objective truth, or indeed with any standards. A price that we have paid for divorcing objective truth from sincerity, is to divorce subjective emotionalism from all discipline – and from community cohesion. We having made truth amoral, the next generation has made self-expression amoralistic also. This makes for social disorder, and for personal loneliness, and lostness. Just as we cannot have a basketball game without honesty, so there can be none without rules. It is a sorry society whose only two activities seem to be organized dishonest contests on the one hand and chaotic, fragmentedly private, bacchanalia on the other.

But of course life is not a game; it is 'for real'. The rules of life must be objectively true – as well as personally right.

Over against the historical argument, some would respond, the theoretical horn of our dilemma remains. It might be 'better' to live in a world of personalist truth: better for us as persons, better for our society, better even for our universities as institutions. Yet if it be not 'truer' then we ought not to choose its comfort over the bleakness, demanding all our courage, of the world as it starkly, impersonally, is.

This consideration is important; and if the dichotomy were valid, my own commitment to truth is such that I too would choose it. (Does this mean, then, that one cannot after all, in dealing with the theoretical issue of what truth is, escape wrestling with the metaphysical issue of what reality [*ḥaqq*] is, as well as the moral issue, as to how one shall personally relate to both? Is it possible, within a logical system that repudiates metaphysical and moral dimensions to truth, to assert that one conception of truth is either truer, or better, than another?) This very consideration, in any case, of whether one should choose truth over comforting illusion, itself begins to bridge the gulf between truth and moral integrity. For the commitment to truth is personal, is moral.

Besides, our argument is not at all that one should choose personal morality rather than objective truth. Those who see the locus of truth and falsity as statements or propositions, are not contending that the only criterion of truth is logical self-consistency. The formulation must be internally coherent, no doubt; but to be true, it must also relate to objective facts in a certain strict fashion. Similarly, to see the locus of truth and falsity as persons is not to contend that honesty or internal integrity is its sole criterion. When truth is seen as personal, a man's statement must not only cohere with his (and if it be about other men, then also with their) inner life, but must also relate to objective facts in that same exacting fashion.

Moreover, the choice that we make is not quite ours to make arbitrarily. Even if it could be shown that personalist and pro-positional conceptions of truth were equally plausible, theoretically (although I do not believe that they are), there are other factors involved. The university that I served has as its motto: *Veritas*. It is cheating a little, the historian may report, if today it interprets that aspiration as towards merely propositional truth, when the word once meant, and Harvard once meant by it, a truth from which health and wholeness and integrity are not precluded. Thus we are not quite at liberty to make the term 'truth' mean whatever we choose to mean by it; for we are trustees in our society of traditions and values and even of terms whose moral as well as intellectual content is at stake. A university unconcerned with personal truth is untrue (*sic*) to the academic tradition, historically, as well as, I submit, sadly partial in its apprehension of intellectual rigour today.

For the conceptual systems that we adopt do themselves, in their entirety, like individual statements within them, have to be related to the world in which we live, and not merely to be internally consistent. The medieval Islamic, Christian, Hindu Weltanschauungen were once mighty orientations but today they serve no longer so well because, however coherent in themselves and however true to personal inner life, they have not incorporated (cannot incorporate?) into their structures the new data of modern scientific and historical knowledge. Similarly the conceptual system of amoral proposition-alism, however logically potent, cannot successfully cope with the data, the givenness, of human moral and personal life. A con-ception of truth that is impersonal handles the natural world well, but comprehends the world of man ineptly.

This presentation may not have succeeded in making persuasive the suggestion that advance in our individual and corporate life requires a personalization of our sense of truth, a re-integration of objective rightness and inward rightness. At least I am grateful for the opportunity to have argued for an awareness that little is so important about a culture, or a century, or a person, as his or its vision of truth. Pilate's unanswered question, What is Truth? whether expressed or latent, haunts every civilization, and finally, I guess, every man. We may hope that our society will not cease to wrestle with it earnestly and nobly. In such wrestling, even if we be maimed by it, there may surely be a blessing.

NOTES

1 On the matter of the classical Islamic view of the morality of truth and lies, it is perhaps not inappropriate to quote here something that I had occasion to write elsewhere in commenting on a work of Muḥammad ibn 'Abd al-Karīm al-Shahrastānī (1076-1153) who in a particular passage 'contends that a false sentence is not in-trinsically better or worse, morally, than a true one. Some truths, he says, are not very pretty. (Keats was inspired by an urn to remind us that this view is un-Grecian.) There are some who would agree with this, holding that it is not lies themselves, but the telling of lies, that is wrong. Our author goes further: for him, the telling of lies, even, is not intrinsically moral or immoral. What is wrong, hellishly so, is for *me* to tell a lie – or for you to do so. And the reason for this is that God has created us and has commanded us not to lie.' In: George A. Makdisi, ed., *Arabic and Islamic Studies in Honor of Hamilton A. R. Gibb*, (Leiden, Brill, 1965), p. 598.

2 And what eternity is all about, too, in a sense. The reality of the objective world, although it is prior to our personal orientation to that reality, yet in the end will vanish while the way that you and I have responded to that reality is of a transcending significance which, to use the poetic imagery, will survive, will cosmically outlast the world. The mundane world is independent of man and is not to be subordinated to his whimsies. Yet ultimately, in this vision, man, if he relates himself truly to reality, is greater than the world.

3 I say 'trilateral' because in the case of, for instance, a statement, three things are involved: the man who makes the statement, the statement itself, and the facts that it purports to describe. (In a game, cheating similarly involves three things: the cheater, his action, and the rules of the game.) I leave aside for the moment a question (in the end, perhaps exceedingly important) as to whether we should in fact include a fourth element in the complex: the person spoken to, the other player. The common view that the truth of a statement is a function of the relation between it and the overt facts may be termed a bilateral theory. (A relationship cannot be unilateral.)

4 *Quawm kānū ṣadaqū bi-alsinatihim, wa-lam yuṣaddiqū qawlahum bi-fi'lihim.* Literally: 'A people who used to give *ṣidq* with their tongues, but did not give *taṣdīq* to what they said by their action'. Abū Ja'far Muḥammad ibn Jarīr al-Ṭabari, *Jāmi' al-Bayān fī Tafsīr al-Qur'ān*, ad 49:14.

5 The Islamic epistemological point that Muslims learn what the final truth is about man's duty and destiny through the divine disclosure of it (in their case, in the Qur'ān) was of course taken for granted in the theological treatises, and eventually colours the further discussion of faith a little, though surprisingly little. As my presentation has perhaps made clear and as a book on which I am working will more explicitly document, a sizeable portion of many passages in Islamic theology about faith could be introduced word for word in Christian discussions of the matter almost without modification, and with considerable profit. And the same might be true, to some degree, in humanist discussions.

Originally the intention was that this present paper was to have been entitled 'Where Lies Religious Truth?', and was to develop specifically the view that the locus of *religious* truth is persons. The argument would have elaborated the consideration of the *taṣdīq* conceptualization, for the Islamic case, and would have endeavoured to systematize theoretically the personalist-truth notions set forth in my recent work *Questions of Religious Truth* (Gollancz, 1967). In tackling this, however, I found myself increasingly disquieted with the notion that *any* truth about men, whether religious or other, can be localized in a proposition; and I found myself writing instead this present, less satisfactory but I suppose more provocative, paper. Perhaps a sober position might finally be that truth or falsity, in this realm, is a function not of a proposition only but of it and of the person who makes it, but that there is perhaps a range of types of proposition, with the personalist element being lowest (or merely: most universal?) when the proposition refers to natural-science matters, higher when it refers to social-science matters, very high in various special cases, and highest in the religious realm. For another day, perhaps.

6 I am not arguing here that with the propositional-truth notion one cannot cope with personalisms as a special case – just as I trust that my critics will not suppose that with the personalist view being proposed it would be impossible to accommodate, again as a rather special case, certain impersonal objectivisms. The question is rather one of where one puts primacy. And especially, of where one puts aspiration – not merely individually but socially, institutionally (as we consider *infra*, about Harvard's aspiration).

With the diffidence of an outsider in these matters, I venture to ponder some of Austin's handling of this particular issue in my next note.

7 An outsider dare not but be tentative and diffident in these matters; one of the great advantages accruing, along with the honour that is done, in being invited to a conference of philosophers of this sort, is that one may hope for swift correction when one intrudes into the domain of the specialists. I dare venture into this area at all only, apart from the invitation, because I see the issues as not strictly within philosophy – at least, not philosophy as contemporarily understood – but rather as having to do with the relation between philosophy and culture, and that between culture and human life (understood historically, but in a way transcending Western, and especially modern Western, particularities, for those who wish to remain empirical; understood in ultimate or absolute or religious terms, for those who allow these).

First, then, is it fanciful to raise a perhaps innocent inquiry regarding Wittgenstein's famous problem of games? One may ask what all those things called 'game' have in common, and find nothing; may press one's modern fellows to search and scutinize and *look* at games to see what indeed they have in common; may perhaps be a whit disparaging when, although they cannot find such a thing objectively there, they yet continue to feel uneasily that 'they must have something in common because we call them all games'. May one have missed something at once both simple and im-portant? May it not be that what all games have in common is the simple fact that men call them all games? What characterizes them all, despite their diversity, is that we human beings are related to them in a particular way. And this relationship is profoundly im-portant. Modern men do not see it because they are looking in the wrong place. The ruthless insistence that the proper way, the only way, to understand the world is to see it apart from man's relation to it, may not be so legitimate as some have thought. This principle of 'objectivity' may lead, or have led, to something reasonably called truth in the natural sciences, but I ponder the possibility that it may lead to error in the 'behavioural' sciences and in all our apprehension of things that pertain to man. On another occasion I have defined 'objectivity' as the proper way to handle objects intellectually; but to treat men, or anything involving men, as if they were objects is to misunderstand them.

Might one propose: nothing that men do can be adequately understood objectively?

Might one further raise a question also about Austin, and even perhaps speculate whether his views do not in some fashion lend surreptitious support to such a proposal? Although here again I feel highly diffident in exposing my uncouthness in the unfamiliar field of modern philosophy, I venture to trespass in that field if only to profit from expert comment. An outsider's questions may sound inept, but through them the questioner, at least, may win some light. With regard to Austin's essay 'Truth', my unsophisticated feeling is that he comes close to being a moralist and personalist, but would shy away from formulating his position so. His notion of 'statement', for example (as distinct from a sentence), which seems certainly non-empirical, non-'objective', appears strikingly supernatural unless it be interpreted as an implicitly personalist conception. Indeed it is of something said 'by a certain person' (p. 87), and when two persons use the same sentence it may make two statements, one for each (p. 88). Moreover he was clearly fascinated with promises, and stressed the moral-personal dimension even of knowing (e.g., in 'Other Minds'). On some points, however, he was unwilling to be personalist: for example, for him 'that cat may be on the mat' (I prefer 'I love you' as a paradigm for truth or falsity!) 'is not a statement' and cannot be true or false (p. 100). Is it, however, unreasonable much to prefer the Arabic dictionaries' notion that when a man says something of that kind, he may be lying or he may be telling the truth?

Moreover, an outsider wonders whether Austin is being perhaps a trifle facile in the way that he tosses off the point that the sentence 'It is mine' may make different statements, depending on who makes it. He does not seem to be concerned with how profoundly personalist he is thereby constituting his concept of 'statement' to be. Whether 'It is mine' is true or false, depends *both* on who says it, *and* on certain objective matters. It seems worth pondering whether religious pronouncements are not of this kind (and I am even suggesting, perhaps in the end all pronouncements). Some thinkers, having discovered that religious sentences (and in this they are like more conspicuously personal sentences, such as 'I am twenty years old') are not true or false in themselves, considered objectively, have gone on to assert that they are then meaningless – or that they merely express emotions. Now the sentence 'I am twenty years old' is, I suppose, strictly meaningless, considered in and of itself (also: 'He is twenty years old'). It becomes a meaningful statement when considered in relation to particular persons; the truth of it, however, still depends on its relation, then, to matters in the objective, empirical world. (Without developing the point, I think that it could be argued that even scientific statements are meaningless in and of themselves; their truth comes into significance when related to persons, but in their case the persons are not *particular* persons but all mankind, in principle – at least, provided that they understand the language being used.) Religious formulations, so far as I can see, are perhaps analogous, in relation not so strictly to particular individuals, although that remains, but first to communities. In the course of teaching Islamic and Hindu ideas, I have had the experience of observing how they seem at first 'meaningless' to outsiders; although it is obviously absurd to adjudge meaningless simply what one cannot understand.

8 This point, so far as religious formulations are concerned (and specifically the proposition 'The Qur'ān is the word of God'), is explored in my *Questions of Religious Truth* (op. cit.).

9 This introduces the fourth component in what would become, then, a quadrilateral relationship in which truth is involved (ref. 3).

10 Relevant to the last two considerations is the concept of 'discipline'. This is not precisely defined, and there are a few aspects of the notion that are perhaps valuable, and could be salvaged. Yet one of the questions that I find myself asking – and I am not unaware that this is bold – is whether in general this concept, increasingly dominant in Western intellectual life, has not with its concomitants constituted a formidable disruption. It has largely replaced 'subject-matter' as the operative concept in much university study; and particularly perhaps in the United States it ramifies into and controls a frighteningly large part of what a university does and how it does it. I realize, accordingly, that to question it may appear not merely radical but ridiculous, inane. I do so, however, seriously and responsibly. I have come deeply to feel that the transition from 'subject' to 'discipline' may have constituted a major step in that profoundly wrong turn that has been taken by Western intellectual life somewhere along the line, in the course of the last many decades. Again, this concept may be legitimate in the natural

sciences, but in the study of human affairs it is, I think that I discern, intellectually an error. To write only for one's peers in a discipline is to write not only jargon but – in principle – falsehood; or at least, not truth.

11 In this case the personal morality might be not simply or perhaps even primarily the personal integrity in relation to his work of the individual researcher (although that would be interesting to discuss) but, given the universalist quality of scientific statements, rather or also the group morality of mankind.

12 *Tawḥīd*, to use another Islamic term.

WILFRED CANTWELL SMITH, formerly Professor of World Religions at Harvard University and Director of the Centre for the Study of World Religions, is now McCulloch Professor of Religion, and Chairman of the Department of Religion, Dalhousie University, Canada. He is the author of *Islam in Modern History*; *Modern Islam in India*; *The Meaning and End of Religion*; *The Faith of Other Men*; *Questions of Religious Truth*, etc.

Truth and Religions

NINIAN SMART

This paper contains three parts.[1] The second part, which is the bulk of the paper, asks the question 'Is there a problem about how the truth-claims of Christianity can be reconciled with those of other religions?' The first part sets the ground for the use of certain concepts used in the main part. In particular it attempts to justify, against recent criticism, the use of such terms as 'Christianity', 'a religion', and so on. The third part takes up a particular description of piety (that of Cantwell Smith) in order to show that questions of truth cannot be sidestepped.

It is perhaps worth remarking that one of the very few attempts to deal with questions of criteria of truth, in the inter-religious context, is my own *Reasons and Faiths* (1958). The book is highly defective, and I only mention it because so few people in the field of religious studies have addressed themselves to the problem of criteria, as distinguished from the lower-order exercise of theologizing, dialoguing and the like. Of course, I do not myself think that questions of truth should be dealt with in the abstract, and I am sympathetic in any case to lowering Christian-theological (missiological) temperatures in relation to truth-questions – being convinced on philosophical-historical religious grounds that theologians and missiologists miss the main truth-issues, for the reason of neglect of criteria, and also being convinced on Christian grounds of the necessity to combat arrogance.

Is there a Problem about Religion?

In the following section, I shall make some use of terms such as 'Christianity', 'Buddhism', 'a religion', etc. Understandably, such notions have been criticized of late, e.g. by W. Cantwell Smith in *The Meaning and End of Religion*. The charge briefly is two-fold: first that 'religion' is a confused concept; second that 'a religion' is also (e.g. when reified as Buddhism, Islam, Christianity). The objections are confused, but more on the second issue than the first.

As to the first:

(1) Because we use the word 'religion' it does not follow that there is a common core. Compare 'sport', 'entertainment' – legitimate locutions.

(2) Even if 'religion' cannot be defined (though I believe it can), it does not matter much (can we define 'of', 'red', etc.?)

(3) Cantwell Smith, for example, knocks out 'religion' and 'religions' by replacing them with cumulative traditions and faiths. He writes (p. 155, *op. cit.*): 'This is not the place to enter on a systematic study of faith's expressions.' But this terminology implies as much reification as 'religion' and 'religions'.

More importantly, regarding the possibility of speaking of 'a religion' (e.g. Christianity):

1. The fact that new terms are used (e.g. 'Sikhism') in the modern context does not show that they are inapplicable. The non-traditional nature of western terms does not *by itself* mean that there is a distorting reification. 'Gamesmanship' is of fairly recent coinage, but gamesmanship preceded the coinage (hence the success of the coinage).

2. The fact that an 'ism' does not apply to, say, traditional 'Hinduism' does not mean that it does not in principle apply elsewhere, or to some aspects of modern Indian religion.

3. If people believe that they trace their 'origins' to a single source (Christ, the Buddha, etc.), then there is a reason to define their belief and practice by reference to the source (cp. the use of *Bauddha* in the Indian tradition).

4. In intercultural contact there is a tendency for traditions to precisify their nature (cp. modern Hinduism).

5. It does not follow from the above that one needs to use terms such as 'polytheism', 'monotheism', etc., to categorize religious affirmations – there is no religion called 'polytheism'. One must distinguish between the general issue and the problems arising from western methods of analysis.

6. It is possible that attacks on the notion of 'a religion' arise from a kind of individualism, since superficially the concepts of 'being faithful', 'having faith', 'being committed', etc., apply primarily to individuals. But first this is doubtful (the attention to the first person singular in western philosophy being possibly a legacy of Protestantism) and second these concepts do not, in any case, have universal application (see above, re *faith*).

Having said all this, I am far from denying that there are

problems about what a religion is, and these are partly explored in the next section.

Is there a Problem about how the Truth-Claims of Christianity can be Reconciled with those of other Religions?

The first question about the question is about truth-claims. Not just *truth*-claims, surely? There can be imperatival incompatibilities Religions appear to recommend or command different paths. For the Christian pacifist, 'Turn the other cheek' is vitally right; for the Muslim, it is better to say something like 'Act honourably, but there is no need to turn the other cheek.' Again, different rituals are commended or commanded. For the Catholic, the Mass; for the Muslim, daily prayers and the pilgrimage to Mecca.

So we are not merely concerned with possible incompatibilities as to truth-claims; but also with possible incompatibilities in *practice*-claims.

The next problem about the question has to do with the *identification* of truth-claims and practice-claims as being Christian. The Christian tradition is variegated, as we all know; and we need no reminding that in this age as in many previous epochs Christianity is in flux. It is highly fluctuating in regard to theology, as it happens. How then do we identify the core of Christian truth-claims?

We sometimes operate on the assumption that though there are many Christianities there is only one Christian faith. Thus the great task of theology is to penetrate to this one faith and articulate it and express it. This assumption of the single faith is unaffected by the recognition that there are changing cultural circumstances – that modern man, for instance, may find some elements of traditional expression of the faith (miracle stories, for instance) unacceptable. The programme of demythologization itself is a phase in the never-ending supposed task of relating the one faith to the changing cultural milieu. It is a case of adapting the one to the many. Different times, different theologies – but always the one faith. Different climes, different theologies – but always the one faith. This is the pervasive model at the back of our minds, when we ask about the compatibility or otherwise of Christian truth-claims and those of other faiths. Similar remarks apply, perhaps, to the practice-claims: there is, so to say, a single divine imperative, could we but find it.

The model of a single faith is reinforced by the historical accident (or is it an accident?) that the churches recognize in the New Testament the single platform upon which they all stand. The task of the theologian then becomes importantly to extract the single faith from its pages. Paul here stands as a looming figure, for the more the historicity of the Gospels is called in question (and a century and a half of scientific history is bound to plaster the text with queries), the greater the significance of the great theologian of the risen Christ.

Naturally, there is a similar question about other faiths. Is there a single substance of the Buddhist dharma, for instance? Even in Islam, pegged to the glorious revelation of the Qur'ān, there are variations, developments. Is there then a single Islam?

The question of identifying the one faith in Christianity is made harder by a feeling that often accompanies the model of the one faith – namely that necessarily the focus of faith transcends the concepts which we use to try to express it. If it were not so, the task of identifying the one faith might not be too hard. For one could ask: If Augustine, Aquinas, Luther, and Barth each expressed, in differing cultural milieus, the one faith, then let us state that faith and see the correlation. But it seems that each new theology takes a given core of faith and then elaborates it; rather each new theology is an expression of the theology-transcending X. There is, so to say, no going behind each theology to discover what it is about. It tells you what it is about; it is so to say the glass through which we see the X, and the X can only be seen through one glass or another. If this is so, then the 'one faith' is very much a construct, and one without content. In this respect, the quest of the historical Jesus has been a way of trying to get back to a content, round the glasses which filter our vision.

If what I have said on this score is correct, it presents us with one way of talking about Christian truth- and practice-claims, namely to take the whole exhibition of coloured windows through which the Christian tradition has looked out and back on the theology-transcending focus of faith. Or if it be not possible to treat seriously the whole gallery of theologies, then at least a selection of them. However, the very fact (if it is so) that the focus of faith transcends theologies means that the theological traditions can never be fixed. What is to preclude a new theology being devised, to set alongside the others? In this case, though, there is one sort of identification question which can profitably be asked, namely what is the norm whereby some new theology is adjudged to be *Christian*? Some resemblance, presumably, to earlier theologies. But how much? These things seem to be settled by an informal method of acceptance in the community. For example, Paul van Buren's *The Secular Meaning of the Gospel* expresses an atheistic Christology; but a number of Christians took this with sufficient seriousness to deem it as genuinely a *Christian* theology, despite its formal atheism.

Since new theologies await us over the horizon, it is also necessary to recall that the very situation of interplay between religions, which so markedly characterizes contemporary religious culture, may itself have an impact on theologizing: so that a new theology now beyond the horizon might in theory dissolve some of the incompatibilities between earlier theologies and received non-Christian theologies. For instance, there seems to be a conflict of *Weltanschauung* between theistic Christianity and non-theistic Buddhism; but the incompatibility is less obvious the more Existentialist Christian theology becomes. So new syntheses may await us over the horizon; and they cannot be ruled out *a priori*.

However, there is another check upon indiscriminate synthesizing; this arises from the relation between truth-claims and practice-claims (to put it crudely). It is very obvious that the ritual, experiential and institutional aspects of a religion, and its ethical prescriptions, are not always well co-ordinated to the theologies being purveyed within it. For example, the meaning of the Eucharist, in Anglicanism, is shaped by the milieu of liturgy, architecture, custom, style of life of those engaged: it is not merely determined theologically, still less by the most *avant garde* theology. Attitudes to the Buddha in Theravāda Buddhism are not simply determined by doctrines, but by the whole temple-cultus, etc. Thus there is always the possibility of a lack of co-ordination between truth-claims, and actual practice-claims. In one way, this is doubtless a good thing, for it might be held to be the task of the theologian to criticize, where necessary, the actual practices of the church. But how is this legitimate critical tension to be preserved while at the same time theology is to escape the charge of disingenuousness? For it is a cheat if the theologian does not relate the ideal church to the actual church – if he recommends a faith that has no purchase on the received tradition.

For these and other reasons, the question of incompatibilities between one faith and another is a complex matter. In a way we are concerned with the elasticity of a faith – whether certain kinds of stretching the concepts and practices result in a snap. Let us try out a thought-experiment here, by considering what is to be said about Hindu attitudes to Christianity.

The modern Hindu ideology, if one may so dub it, consists in a neo-Śankaran theology in which all religions, albeit existing at different levels, ultimately point to the one truth. This is an appealing doctrine to many; for it suggests that religions are held apart by externals, institutional narrownesses, rather than by any essential conflict. It is the obverse of the conclusion sometimes drawn from conflicts of revelations and teachings, namely that they are all false; the modern Hindu ideology declares that they are all true. The best religion, however, is one which is explicitly synthesizing, all-embracing (this being the merit of Hinduism). It follows from the modern Hindu ideology that there is no incompatibility between Hinduism and Christianity: they both ultimately have the same focus, though symbolized and concretized differently (Christ and Krishna, for example, are different manifestations of the one God). Should Christianity resist this synthesis? Not just on the ground that the Christian tradition is unique – for every tradition is. Let us consider some of the reasons for resisting the synthesis that might be advanced.

'The Hindu conception of deity is different from that revealed to the Christian tradition.' *Comment*: it is true that God in the main Christian tradition is conceived in a more personal way than is the neo-Advaitin *Brahman*; but in *this* respect the ultimate reality of Tillich and John Robinson is similarly 'impersonal' (compare also pseudo-Dionysius, Meister Eckhart, Dean Mansel). The anti-synthesis argument thus becomes a means of shutting off certain kinds of theological development within Christianity.

'Christ is uniquely Son of God: there are no other incarnations.' *Comment*: this point can be stated if there is a prior monotheism and an identification of sorts of Christ with the one God; but the anti-synthesis argument here will not work in the following conditions: (i) if Christ is seen as a 'window on ultimate reality' (for there can be many windows); (ii) if Christ is seen, liberal theology-wise, as an examplar of moral values (for there could be other exemplars, such as the Buddha); (iii) if Christ is simply the preached Christ – the historical anchor of an imperatival *kerygma* (for there could be a variety of other historical and mystical anchors of existential challenge). In brief, the appeal to the uniqueness of the incarnation implies a rather conservative ontology. But can't it somehow be done by making a practice-claim? Thus:

'Christ alone is to be worshipped.' The Hindu synthesis here seems to be rejected (unless secretly Krishna and others can be *identified* with Christ: to this sort of identification theme we shall return). *Comment*: the practice-claim could simply be a surd imperative, like a surd revelation. But it is usual in the Christian tradition to advance some grounds for the claim – that the risen Christ provides the key to liberation; that it is through sacramental participation in the death and resurrection of Christ that sin and death are overcome; and negatively that other gods do not have liberating power, are phantasms leading men astray, do not exist. It is thus difficult to give grounds for the practice-claim which does not imply some ontology: some account of the human predicament and of the way in which it is overcome. Historically, moreover, the worship of Christ in part arises from the background of worship of the one God. Here is another respect in which the Christian rejection of synthesis rests upon a particular theism. But as I said earlier, there is no knowing what the future may bring: yet at the present time it seems that Christianity, to maintain its incompatibility with Hinduism, would have to appeal to a particular theism as constituting part of its essence. I shall return to this point after a brief excursus on the paradox of a situation in which incompatibility is regarded as a good thing.

Why should there be a motive for standing out against the noble Hindu synthesis? It is partly a matter of having a *raison d'être*. A movement, religious or otherwise, which does not have a distinctive message tends (rightly) to wither. Still, couldn't Christianity have a more modest *raison d'être* – to nurture those within it and those who find that it chimes in with their spiritual and moral condition? It could be, so to speak, a loosely knit tribal religion, but where the tribe is a new Israel, not ethnically determined (although well rooted in certain, mainly western cultures). One must here, however, understand the logical and cultural predicament of a tribal religion in an intercultural situation (this too will cast light upon the reason for the evolution of the new Hindu ideology).

A tribal religion, like other religions, contains a doctrinal element, woven into the whole practical side: a certain picture of the world and of spirit is drawn. Consider the predicament of the tribal folk when it is faced with a new culture, with a transethnic religion. Is it possible for the tribal folk long to maintain that their world-picture is for them, the other world-picture for others? It is hard to say (from a logical point of view) that P is true for one group and not-*P* for another, unless all that is meant is that the one group *believes P* and the other believes not-*P*. Various devices have to be employed if the tribal picture is to remain itself at all. One option is hard – to claim that the tribal picture is of universal validity, for it was always meant for those initiated into tribal lore, and wasn't meant at all for other tribes. This secretive non-universalism could be carried with equanimity when the tribe constituted the real world, the values of other men being a mere shadowy penumbra. Even very big groups have felt like this: for the Chinese, barbarian values were shadowy until Buddhism crept in and destroyed the illusion; for expansionist Europe, the beliefs of colonized folk tended to be curiosities, oddities; in India over a long period the real world was the subcontinent, until Buddhism began to flicker outwards. So then our tribal folk will find the universalist option hard to maintain, because of the tight connection between the picture of the world and the secret sacraments of the tribe. Another option it may not want to face – namely to abandon entirely its own picture and assimilate that of the new culture, though even here unconsciously the old gods can be smuggled in. A *via media* is called for: one in which an adjusted world-picture is seen as a contribution to the store of myths and insights which point towards transcendent. We may call this option: unity through conscious pluralism, or in short 'the pluralistic solution'.

We can now return to the question of whether Christianity can regard itself modestly as a loosely-knit tribal religion, nurturing those who participate in its sacraments. Faced with other trans-cultural faiths, it would be essentially in the tribal predicament, if so; and truth is no respecter of groups. To retain its modesty, without losing its *raison d'être*, it would have itself to adopt the pluralistic solution, and this would be virtually to accept the Hindu synthesis. In the context of the variety of faiths and of the virtual certainty that they will continue substantially in a plural world, the pluralistic solution seems sound common sense. Hence its appeal (a wide appeal, even among many Christians, who express this pluralism through a scepticism about missions, though not about hospitals in alien climes).

I have made something in this argument of the tightness of the connection between the tribal world-picture and their secret sacraments. This point is highly relevant to problems of meaning and understanding. Crudely one can distinguish between an initiatory and a non-initiatory view of understanding religious concepts. From the initiatory point of view, understanding God can only be approached via the sacramental or analogous activities, or can only be gained by the initiation constituted by the experience of grace. Full-bloodedly, the initiatory view is a sort of conceptual fideism: only those who can say 'I know that my redeemer liveth' know what 'redeemer' means. A thin-blooded view would be that we can imaginatively enter into initiations (hence the possibility of coming to understand something of other faiths). Those espousing a hardheaded natural theology would hold that at least some key concepts in religion could be understood metaphysically, without specific religious initiation.

There is a tension here. The more conceptually initiatory a religion is, the more it takes on the character of a tribal religion, except that it may be the religion of an open rather than a closed tribe, adding new members as it can. But though it could be thus universal evangelically, in the sense that any man or all men might join the faith-community, it could, if thus conceptually initiatory, give no reasons why men should join, save 'Come and see', maybe. In *practice*, of course, men who join use reasons: the fruits are good – you can see peace on their faces, and so forth. This is a kind of practical natural theology, adding some rationality to the otherwise surd initiation. But by contrast, if a religion seems to be hardly initiatory at all, for the understanding of its concepts, it takes on the guise of a metaphysics, and the link between belief and sacrament is ruptured.

Extreme conceptual fideism as an account of the Christian faith does, I think, have to be rejected, if the aim at any rate is to avoid the pluralistic solution. For paradoxically conceptual fideism can give no account of what other faiths mean (e.g. the Hindu synthesis): for it is implied that initiation is necessary for understanding. Given the further premiss that one cannot be initiated properly into more than one faith (*pace* Ramakrishna), then the Christian conceptual fideist can have no ground for rejecting any other faith. All faiths have this rather negative equal status. This being so, there can be no reason to reject the Hindu claim that all faiths point to the same Truth. Initiatory conceptual fideism slides in to acceptance of a polytheism, or rather a polyfideism, if one may coin so barbarous a hybrid.

But *should* the extra premise, that one cannot be properly initiated into more than one faith, be accepted? Is it that no man can serve two masters? But how are we to know that they *are* two masters? Is it that a person cannot be converted from one faith to another? We know that this happens empirically, so to speak; but could he really have had his earlier faith if he were converted? These are questions which extreme conceptual fideism is not in a position to answer.

As a postscript to the discussion of extreme conceptual fideism, it is worth noting that whereas truth and falsity do not admit, in any straightforward way, at least, of degrees, understanding does. One person can show greater, deeper, etc., understanding than another. It may be that a very deep understanding of the concepts of a given faith is not accessible to the adherent of another faith; but this does not at all show that *some* level of understanding is impossible for him; and it can of course well be that the adherent of a faith has a less profound understanding of it than some person of another faith.

The pluralistic solution, as we have outlined it, is not absolute pluralism: there is at least the notion that there is a single truth towards which different religions point – in line with the modern Hindu ideology, which itself constitutes the response of a sophisticated, variegated cultural tradition faced by an incoming transethnic faith, accompanied by aggressive European values. This attempt at making differing traditions compatible by postulating a single focus of aspiration does, however, depend on identifications – identifying one divine focus of faith with another. Can such identifications be justified?

Let us begin with a relatively simple example. What justifies one in saying that the Christian and Muslim worship the same God? As far as the concepts and practices go, the two foci of faith are different. Among other things, the Christian worships Christ as a person of the Trinity: the Christian concept of God is thus organically related to God's manifestation in history and to his representation of himself in the sacraments. These are elements not present in the Muslim's conception of Allah. Thus conceptually the Christian God and Allah are different. This does not entail that the concepts do not refer to the same Being: far from it, a major point about identity statements is that the concepts are different (not all identity statements, but many, e.g. 'Tomorrow is Friday'). The statement 'The Christian and the Muslim worship the same God' is not just to be interpreted intentionally, with phenomenological brackets as it were: rather, it is itself a theological statement, assuming the existence of a single God for both Christians and

Muslims to worship. But if it is a theological claim, then from within which tradition? Or does it stand outside both? It could do, e.g., if it is part of the expression of the modern Hindu ideology. But let us consider more narrowly the reasons that a *Christian* theologian might give for the assertion. Let us assume too that he here as elsewhere is presenting a glass through which one can look on the focus of faith – there being no independent access to that focus. The only ground, one supposes, for the identification is that there is a sufficient degree of resemblance between the Christian and Muslim conceptions of God. Since, however, there is a certain degree of elasticity in Christian theology itself, for the focus of faith is theology-transcending, it is unlikely that it would take very strict account of what constitutes a sufficient degree of resemblance.

However, this way of discussing the issue might seem overly conceptual. After all, is it not largely upon the practical side of religion that the theologian feeds? Does his concept of God not articulate what is given in experience, ritual, history? Not surprisingly, those who espouse the pluralistic solution tend to stress the unity of religious *experience*. Thus an important part of the task of trying to establish a sufficient degree of resemblance is the attempt to evaluate the existential and experiential impact of different foci of faith. Strictly, there are two things to do: first, to arrive at a sensible and sensitive phenomenology of religious experience (basically a descriptive task this, though not without its conceptual pitfalls); and second, to see whether the results contribute to the judgement that there is a sufficient degree of resemblance to justify the identification of one focus of faith with another.

The phenomenological judgement as to whether there is a basic common core of religious experience must be based on the facts, and not determined *a priori* by theology. I do not wish to argue the point here: but my own view is that there is no such common core, but rather that there are different sorts of religious experience which recur in different traditions, though not universally. From a phenomenological point of view it is not possible to base the judgement that all religions point to the same truth upon religious *experience*. Nor is it reasonable to think that there is sufficient conceptual resemblance between God and nirvānā (as conceived in Theravāda Buddhism) to aver that the Theravādin and the Christian are worshipping the same God (for one thing, the Theravādin is not basically *worshipping*). Thus it is hard to justify the pluralistic

solution, at least as elaborated in the modern Hindu ideology –
save by saying that Christians and Buddhists are really aspiring
towards the same focus of faith, even though they cannot know that
they are. But what then are the criteria of identity of aspiration?
Is there a conceptual baptism of desire?

In brief, there are problems about the pluralistic solution, mainly
problems of identification of the religious ultimate. It still remains,
however, that there is something to commend the solution: to put
the matter in a nasty nutshell, the more evangelical Christianity is,
the more it approximates to an open tribal faith, for the truth has
to be experienced through the forms of Christian faith; but by the
same token there is less ground for dismissing the truth of other
initiations. On the other hand, the less evangelical Christianity
becomes, the less motive it will have for resisting the pluralistic
solution.

But *still* the argument may be over-conceptual, over-theological.
Can the practical natural theology mentioned earlier come in to
provide the test? It would be something of an irony if human fruits
were invoked to decide the interpretation of divinity. But this is not
a simple affair, as can be imagined; for what counts as fruits is in
part determined by the theologies and the institutions. For example,
a Christian might bring sustenance to villagers by getting things
done, notably by getting folk to hunt birds; but the fruits of
Christian dynamism have to be judged by attitudes to animal life.
The Buddhist might not be unqualified in his praise of the dynamism. This indicates that the problem of compatibility is not just to
do with the religious ultimate, but with the diagnosis of the worldly
situation, including importantly the human situation.

The pluralistic situation is attractive, but it is doubtful whether
it could work in the present state of religious traditions, because it
is phenomenologically unsound. In an important way, then, there is
incompatibility (at present) between religious truth-claims. There is
also divergence in practice-claims. It is a further question as to the
criteria for resolving questions of truth and practice. There are,
however, certainly grounds for arguing both for and against the
monotheism which makes sense of Christ's exclusive claim as
liberator. As I have attempted to argue elsewhere, these criteria
importantly have to do with religious experience and cultus. For
the rest, we must accept that every religion has a given starting
point, each unique. The pictures in the gallery are different, have
different atmospheres and messages; they cannot be aligned in the

same pictorial perspective. And for most men only one picture can be a real focus of loyalty.

How not to Evade Questions of Truth (not that these are all)

In view of the conclusion of the foregoing section, I am clearly in an ambiguous position. What is clear, however, is that simplistic attempts to resolve the question of truth must be criticized, however charitable their intent. One such is W. Cantwell Smith's appeal to faith and God. In *The Meaning and End of Religion* (p. 181), near the final conclusion he writes:

> The end of religion, in the classical sense of its purpose and goal, that to which it points and may lead, is God. Contrariwise, God is the end of religion also in the sense then when He appears vividly before us, in His depth and love and unrelenting truth all else dissolves; or at least religious paraphernalia drop back into their due and mundane place, and the concept 'religion' is brought to an end. This occurs also even when the unrelenting truth is only that of scholarly enquiry.

At the end of his *Questions of Religious Truth* (p. 123) he writes:

> I still hold, then, that there are no nouns. Religious life begins in the fact of God: a fact that includes His initiative, His agony, His love for all of us without discrimination, without favor, without remainder. Given that fact – and it is given; absolutely and quite independently of how we human beings recognize it; given that irremovable fact – religious life then consists in the *quality* of our response.

The two quotations attract the following comments.

1. In the first quotation, 'classical' means 'Western classical'. This is a culture-bound account, therefore.

2. Is Buddhism a religion? If not, let the Buddha *not* appear in indexes of books on religion. If so, then the goal of religion is not necessarily God. It is absurd or at least odd to say that all religions (religious people) believe in God.

3. Once God appears to us, the concept 'religion' is brought to an end, it is alleged. I would think that a person might attend Mass more frequently, and that is a religious activity.

4. Still, the paraphernalia drop back into their *mundane* place, it is alleged, when the religious ultimate is experienced. But experience is mundane. And what *theology* is presupposed by the dis-

tinction between the religious ultimate and the mundane?

5. To associate scholarly enquiry with an implicit theology is in principle all right (where else is Providence?). But it is odd to talk of the 'unrelenting truth' of scholarly inquiry. What is scholarship? Texts? But philosophy can creep in, and that is not *stricto sensu* scholarship. Still less is theology. Presuppositions creep: is it they that do not relent?

It seems that there is still unclarity about the threefold distinction between Christian theology, philosophy, and the scientific study of religion. This is one reason why there is not a sharp view of the problems about the criteria of religious truth.

NOTE

1 Part of this paper was read to the Christian Philosophers' Group in September 1969. The polemical part of the paper is somewhat directed at Professor Cantwell Smith, whose scholarship and writings I much admire, even if I disagree profoundly about some consequences of his theory of religious truth.

NINIAN SMART is Professor of Religious Studies at the University of Lancaster. Author of *Reasons and Faiths*; *A Dialogue of Religions*; *Philosophers and Religious Truth*; *Doctrine and Argument in Indian Philosophy*; *The Yogi and the Devotee*; *The Religious Experience of Mankind*; *Myth, Ritual and Logic*; *The Phenomenon of Religion*; *The Concept of Worship*; *Philosophy of Religion*, etc.

Communalism and
the Social Structure of Religion

TREVOR LING

The Monolithic Concept of 'Religions': a Dissuasive

Among the dangers to the peace of the world today religious communalism might appear to rank as one of the more serious. Such terms as Catholic, Protestant, Muslim, Hindu and the like, have been in the past and still are battle cries, and very effective ones, since they canalize one of the most powerful of emotions, the religious, often in the service of a very powerful animal urge, that of the defence or expansion of one's territory.

Their use, as Wilfred Cantwell Smith[1] has shown us, is relatively recent; it is a feature of modern times. It was in the eighteenth century that the use of the term Christianity became general. In India religious communalism was not inaugurated by British Christians in the nineteenth century, but it was they who insisted on drawing such attention to it as to make Indians more religiously-community minded. In so doing they drove a wedge not only between Christians on the one hand and Hindus and Muslims on the other, but also between Hindus and Muslims, alienating one Indian community from another. Lord Canning, Viceroy of India at the time of the Sepoy revolt of 1857, wrote to Queen Victoria describing the attitude of most of his fellow countrymen in India. There is, he wrote, 'a rabid and indiscriminating vindictiveness abroad, even amongst many who ought to set a better example, which it is impossible to contemplate without something like a feeling of shame for one's fellow countrymen'. If it be objected that it was as British colonists and not as Christians that they adopted such attitudes the answer is that this is *not* how they saw it, according to Canning. It was as Englishmen *and Christians* that they were so conscious of their superiority. 'That which they desire to see is a broad line of separation, and of declared distrust drawn between us Englishmen and every subject of your Majesty who is not a Christian, and who has a dark skin.'[2] The systematic reign of terror lasting for four months up to February 1858, during which British soldiers 'literally drunk with plunder', as *The Times* correspondent put it, sacked and spoiled and wrought revenge, was not enough for Outram; he was for razing the entire city of Delhi to the ground, or if not this, at least the Great Mosque. Here was the heart of the matter in his view; such an act of destruction would, he wrote in January 1858, 'be a heavy blow to the Mahomedan religion'.[3] In the presence of such English religious-communal zeal Canning's firm sense of justice was infuriating to his fellow countrymen; they labelled him 'Clemency Canning' and petitioned the queen for his removal from India. Contrasts were frequently made by the British in India from this time onwards between Christianity on the one hand, and Hinduism and Islam on the other, in terms of superiority and inferiority, moral and cultural: it was as simple as that. Well might Queen Victoria, after the Revolt, issue a proclamation to the effect that none of her Indian subjects should be 'in any wise favoured, none molested or disquieted by reason of their religious faith or observance,' but by this time there was abundant evidence of contrary intention among the Christian British, especially towards Muslims. One factor in nineteenth century Indian history which, perhaps more than any other, set Muslim communalism on its feet and marching – towards the bloody surgery of India in 1947 – was this nineteenth century English Christian attitude of superiority and contempt towards Muslims.

The dangers are still with us, greatly enhanced. Judgements on other faiths are made, not out of quiet reflection upon evidence that has been carefully weighed, but on purely partisan grounds. Among Christians there is very often a strong devotion and real belief in something they consider can be identified by the word 'Christianity'.

Now it may be objected that this complaint is unreasonable, since it is only to be expected, or even to be desired that a man should show loyalty to the religious system to which he belongs. But to what 'religious system' do such Christians belong? Or to what 'religious system' can the term Christianity be satisfactorily applied? The irony of the situation is that quite often the term Christianity is used by those who belong to a tradition that is alien to the presuppositions of this term, that is, a tradition which is *not* that of the all-dominant, adherence-demanding macro-system. Very often they belong to a line that originally stood out against monolithic religion, affirming the spiritual integrity of each congregation of believers, committed to thoughtful independent judgement on matters of controversy and 'in all things, charity'. Nowadays, many of them appear to have become Christian organization men, the dupes of Christian ecumenism, dedicated to the advancement of an ill-defined if not undefinable entity called Christianity.

Even at a superficial level it is evident that terms such as Christianity, Hinduism, etc., are of little heuristic value. The fact that such terms have been invented and have gained currency is no guarantee that they refer to real objective recognizable entities, each possessing a sufficiently high degree of internal unity to justify the degree of external differentiation which the terms imply. The word Christianity, for instance, is required to do duty for such a wide range of meanings that, as soon as any serious discussion begins, one is forced to ask 'What *sort* of Christianity do you mean?' This can be seen most readily in connection with statements that Christianity 'teaches' this or that. When such an assertion is made, it immediately becomes necessary to ask, 'Do you mean that this is taught by Catholics, or by Calvinists, or by Pentecostalists, etc.? Or are you claiming that it is taught by all of these?' The number of assertions to which a positive answer to the latter question could be given would be very small. The doctrine that God is entirely omnipotent and in his omnipotence predestines some men for eternal salvation and others for damnation may be central to Calvinistic theology, but it can hardly be said to be a doctrine which is central to all the religions which tend to be lumped under the name 'Christianity'. One cannot therefore say Christianity teaches that doctrine unless one is prepared also to say that whatever supposedly Christian bodies do not affirm this doctrine are not to be included within the scope of the term 'Christianity'. In that case, the term is seen to vary in meaning from speaker to speaker. According to whether a man is Greek Orthodox, Roman Catholic, Plymouth Brother, Salvationist, Quaker, Anglican, evangelical fundamentalist, or any other of the list of possibilities – so he will inject his own meaning into the term. The question that then arises, which of them is right? is beside the point. For the point is, that little can with confidence be predicated of this hypothetical 'Christianity', except at a level so general and superficial as to be worthless, if human speech is to have any value.

In case it should be thought that 'Christianity' has been singled out unfairly, or is a special case, it may be worthwhile to mention that the situation is similar in the case of other such terms. 'Hinduism' for example, a western neologism, has no genuine equivalent in the languages of India. There is the term *sanatāna dharma*, but who is to say which of the six or more main meanings of *dharma* is intended here, especially when qualified by *sanatāna*? More cogently one may ask whether 'Hinduism' is a term that embraces the religion of those who accept the authority of the *Veda*, the corpus of sacred scripture preserved and transmitted by Brahmans. If so, Vaiṣṇavas and other adherents of bhakti and tantric cults whose attitude to the Veda ranges between ambiguity and indifference would not be included in 'Hinduism'. Approximately the same cleavage would appear over the question whether the caste-system is integral to 'Hinduism' or not. It might then seem that we should reserve the use of the term Hinduism for those elements of Indian religion which are broadly speaking Brahmanical. But in that case why not say what we mean and speak of Brahmanism, for that would clarify discussion considerably, and avoid many of the confusions and ambiguities that plague the Indian public scene where religious issues are concerned?[4]

Certainly the term Buddhism, by itself, has no identifiable referent that I know of. At one extreme there is the Theravāda tradition of the Saṅgha with its strict adherence to the Pāli scriptures, and especially to the Vinaya discipline, such as prevails in Thailand. On the other hand there is the form of tantric religion which, exported from northern India in the early medieval period and blended with elements of the Bon religion, emerged into the modern world as Tibetan Buddhism, with its married monks, its reincarnated bodhisattvas (the Dalai Lamas), who were also supreme temporal rulers, and its acceptance of a vast range of Sanskrit sūtras as the word of the eternal Buddha. Again there is the Pure Land Buddhism of Japan, the cult of the saviour Amida, who by his grace freely saves all men, even the most sinful, who call upon his name in simple trust, and brings them to his eternal paradise. And, again, there is Zen. It is, therefore, very difficult to envisage what single, identifiable, real entity the term 'Buddhism' might refer to.

Another way of seeing the diversity that is comprised within the term 'Christianity', etc., is in terms of an analysis of types of religion offered by Max Weber.[5] The essential nature of religion is that it is a scheme of salvation from whatever are conceived to be the present unsatisfactory conditions of the actual human situation to some desirable transcendent state of being. Important differences can be observed in the ways in which men believe that this is effected, in other words, between types of soteriology. Weber identifies certain major types. Among those which have reference to belief in a God there are three. All agree that salvation is due to the grace of the god; they differ in their conceptions of how this grace is made available to men. In one case, which Weber calls the sacramental, grace is understood as being made available through the agency of an institution, divinely ordained for the purpose. This type Weber describes as 'institutional grace' (*Anstaltsgnade*), where the divine grace which is the means of salvation is distributed by the official representatives of the divinely ordained system. Examples of this type would be the Brahmanical sacrificial cultus in India, and the Roman Catholic Church. A principle necessarily involved here is: *extra ecclesiam nulla salus*; salvation cannot be obtained apart from or outside of the institution or order which has been vested with the control of grace. A second major type is that in which grace is bestowed freely by a heavenly saviour upon the devotee; his own willingness to accept the saviour's grace is the only condition for its reception; the relationship is conceived in spiritual terms, between the 'soul' of the responding devotee and the saviour who dwells in the heavenly sphere. Characteristic of this type is passionate devotion to the saviour, an attitude of fervent adoration with which the devotee responds to the divine saviour, a fervour which is expressed in ardent prayer, singing and dancing that may sometimes result in a state of ecstasy of soul. Examples of this type of soteriology are the highly emotional bhakti cults in Śrī Vaiṣṇavism, the Pure Land of Amida cult in Japanese religion, and Christian pietist sects. A third type identified by Weber is that in which grace is made available to men on the basis of divine predestination. In this case salvation is understood to be 'a completely free, inexplicable gift of grace from a god absolutely unsearchable as to his decisions, who is necessarily unchanging because of his omniscience, and utterly beyond the influence of any human behaviour'.[6] Such an understanding of the possiblity of salvation (for some) implies also the possibility of no salvation (for others). It is associated with belief in a certain kind of transcendent creator-god, a majestic king whose regime may appear irrational to human beings but is not to be questioned for it is rational from the point of view of the transcendent god. The grace of predestination is illustrated most clearly in Islam; possibly also in the Tengalai school of south Indian Vaiṣṇavism, and in the now declining number of Christian groups that hold a rigorous doctrine of predestined grace.

Each of these soteriologies has its own characteristic consequences in the realm of personal conduct. Only in the case where salvation is believed to be predestined grace, however, does there result a rational ordering of life (*Lebensgestaltung*), according to Weber. The individual who has accepted the doctrine of predestination is very strongly motivated for following an ethically rationalized pattern of life, for the careful and rigorous patterning of his life in such a way is proper to one who enjoys divine favour. Belief in predestination, Weber argued, 'although it might logically be expected to result in fatalism, produced in its most consistent followers the strongest possible motives for acting in accordance with the god's pattern.'[7] But where grace was secured by sacramental means there was at best only a limited development of a rational plan of life. The continual vouchsafing of grace through the sacramental system, and in particular through the confesional, facilitates the individual's capacity to bear guilt, and thus, says Weber, 'it largely spares him the necessity of developing an individual planned pattern of life based on ethical foundations'.[8] Again, in the case of the pietistic method of receiving grace, by an immediate personal, spiritual relationship with the saviour, there is a 'strong tendency to seek the integration of one's pattern of life in subjective states and in an inner reliance upon God'. This is the more so, the more passionate is the interior devotion to the saviour. So far as the Vaiṣṇavism of Bengal is concerned, evidence of this tendency is provided quite independently of Weber by a modern writer on the history of Bengal, J. C. Ghosh. He writes of the *bhakti* type of pietism that was widespread in the seventeenth and eighteenth centuries: 'Instead of helping its followers to improve the real world in which they lived, it enticed them away' to a world where 'The human soul eternally sought the divine over-soul in mystical ecstasy ... For two centuries the Bengali people, sang, danced, and passed out in ecstatic trance while the world around them remained sunk in ignorance and misery.'[9]

If Weber's identification of three types of salvation religion, each with its consequential effects on the personal conduct of life, is accepted, it will be seen that this is a typology that cuts right across the unity of 'Christianity', and even through 'Protestantism'. For within what has been known as Protestantism there are at least these two main major types – the religion of salvation by predestined grace, with its attendant rational ethic, and the religion of salvation appropriated as a personal relationship with the saviour by all who turn to him in loving devotion, with its attendant emphasis upon the interior spiritual relationship rather than on the ordering of the external world.

There is, however, a notion that 'Protestantism' has a simple, single inner religious logic; this has been urged in modern times, for example, by American sociologists, such as Robert E. Lee, who have spoken of 'common-core Protestantism'. In spite of its fissiparous character where organization is concerned, Protestantism has, so it is argued, a common core of belief and practice that provides it with a potential unity. The *dis*unity that Protestantism actually exhibited was, it is argued, due largely to social class differences manifesting themselves in the guise of denominations. In the American situation, Protestantism no longer suffers this social-class disunity and is thus enabled increasingly to find itself as a basic unity of religious thought and action.

This hypothesis has recently been subjected to empirical investigation by Charles Glock and Rodney Stark, who have produced evidence which suggests that there are important radical cleavages within American Protestantism.[10] On the basis of research covering a wide range of Protestant denominations in the San Francisco Bay area, they have demonstrated the existence of a spectrum of beliefs and practices that has Congregationalism consistently at one extreme and a number of small sects of a Pentecostalist kind equally consistently at the other, with Methodists, Episcopalians close to the Congregational end of the spectrum, and Southern Baptists close to the sects. It is important to notice that Glock and Stark used *five* dimensions of religiosity, and it is in terms of each dimension that this kind of spectrum consistently emerges. The five dimensions are (1) the *experiential*, i.e. the individual believer's own account of his religious life and experience; (2) the *ideological*, i.e. religious belief; (3) the *ritualistic*, i.e. religious practices and observances, public and private; (4) the *intellectual*, i.e. the degree to which the believer is informed about his faith and subjects his beliefs to intellectual scrutiny; and (5) the *consequential*, i.e. the practical effects of religious commitment upon the actual ordering of life in the secular realm, both at the individual and the corporate level. While Protestant denominations can be regarded as forming a continuum of this sort, it is noteworthy that between the beliefs, attitudes, practices, and degree of concern for secular areas of life, the differences between the two extremes of the spectrum amount to fundamental cleavages in most of these matters.

The point has perhaps been sufficiently demonstrated that, even in isolation, each of these terms, 'Christianity', etc., covers such a wide range of meanings that it is a very blunt instrument to have to use in reasonable discourse. This devaluation of words is, however, a minor objection compared to the much greater objections which must be raised against the way we have allowed these blunt instruments to be used in public warfare. It is hard to see how the adherents of 'Christianity', engaged in conflict, or even, to use the more fashionable word, 'encounter', with the adherents of 'Hinduism' could possibly know what they were defending, and against what.

My plea, however, is not merely for an embargo on the use of blunt instruments in public religious encounter simply because they are blunt, and may therefore do a lot of harm. The more serious objection to the use of these terms is that they have been shaped by quasi-political forces and serve quasi-political ends. To put this another way, they arise out of concealed quasi-nationalisms, and they advance concealed quasi-nationalistic causes. In order properly to appreciate this, and to understand more clearly the nature of the situation, and the dangerous role that religious communalism plays, a much more refined analysis is necessary than that which the use of such terms as 'Christianity', etc., can provide.

What is a Religious System?

I am aware that, in view of issues that are currently being debated by sociologists, one can introduce the concept of a 'system' into the sociological analysis of religion only very tentatively. It should be said, therefore, that in raising the question, What constitutes an autonomous religious system? I am principally concerned to discover where one can identify the maximum extent of doctrinal consensus *and* of coherence, doctrinal and practical; and where also are approximately the limits of this coherence, beyond which one would encounter doctrines and practices no longer compatible with those that constitute the area of coherence. The doctrines must be held by consensus of the members of the group, and be consistent with one another, and the practices must in some recognizable degree conform to the doctrines. Perhaps this is asking too much; perhaps this is the pure type of an autonomous religious system to

which no known example fully corresponds. Even so, it may serve
as the norm, and actual religious organizations or groups can be
assessed in terms of their degree of approximation to this pure
type. For it must be emphasized that the sociologist is concerned to
look at religious phenomena as they actually are, not as some
theologians believe they are, or hope they are, or think they could
be, if only Christians, Hindus, etc., would behave as good Christians,
Hindus, etc., *should.*

However, to the objections that have already been raised to the
use of the term 'Christianity', the ecumenically-minded theologian
will reply that in spite of all the admittedly divergent traits that can
be pointed out within what he calls 'the Christian tradition' there
are, nevertheless, certain fundamental and important agreements,
and that these agreements amply justify the use of the comprehensive term 'Christianity'. Common to all the groups that he wishes
to see comprised in this term is, he argues, belief in Jesus as the
Christ, as the son of God, and as the saviour of the world. All those
communities, groups, and churches that hold these beliefs comprise
Christianity. Between acceptance and non-acceptance of these
beliefs runs a clear line of demarcation, and it is this that separates
Christianity from 'other religions'. This is broadly the position
adopted by, for example, the World Council of Churches.

As soon as this argument is tested against one's experience of
actual Christian groups, and the data provided by their literature,
one begins to wonder whose purposes are being served by such
massive over-simplification. For only by veiling the ambiguities in
such an assertion, that is, by pretending that all the bodies concerned
understand the same thing by such a phrase as Jesus is the Christ,
or Jesus is the son of God, or Jesus is the saviour of the world, can
the alleged unanimity be maintained. 'Jesus is the saviour of the
world' is an assertion that gains positive meaning only when other
questions have been answered, notably, 'Saves from what?', 'Saves
to what?' and 'Saves how?'. It is on these questions that disagreements have arisen that were serious enough to have been the causes
of bitter conflicts in the past, or if not the causes, to have been
thought big enough issues to afford legitimacy to conflicts that had
other, non-doctrinal causes. Does Jesus save by defeating the devil?
Or by annulling the power of death to those who believe he has
done so? Or by being accepted as a substitute victim whom God
will receive as a sacrifice made in lieu of the whole sinful human
race? Or in lieu of those individual sinful members of the human

race who contritely acknowledge Jesus as the performer of such a role? Christian doctrines of atonement are many, and they are not all mutually reconcilable. A conflate Christian 'doctrine of the atonement' that all would readily accept has yet to be constructed. The same is true of the ways in which Christians have tried to explain what could be meant by the assertions 'Jesus is the son of God', and 'Jesus is the Christ', or 'Jesus is Lord'. If it is so manifestly difficult to obtain agreement on the *meaning* of these assertions, one wonders what value there can be in setting them up as the standards of reference for the alleged overall unity of 'Christianity'. There is, moreover, a considerable naïvety in the notion that real unity is constituted of the obtaining of assent to a few unexplained, ambiguous verbal propositions; it is a mark of an excessively intellectualist stance to believe that somewhere here there will be found a unity strong enough to withstand even the first puff of wind that blows from such grossly materialistic quarters as group prestige, economic interest, political persuasion, or imperialistic intent. The history of Europe and Asia throws severe doubt on the value of this unity from *such* assent to theological propositions, even could it be obtained.

The religious organization that comes nearest to the ideal type of completely unitary structure of belief *and* action is the sect. By this is meant, of course, the sect in its primary form as a voluntary association of likeminded people who come together on the basis of an identity of belief, and of attitudes regarding the courses of action that follow from belief. This is the sect in the first generation, before children have been born to its members and brought up within the sect. Such children may identify themselves with the beliefs and attitudes of the sect, or not. If they do not they either effect a change in the original nature of the sect's beliefs and attitudes (assuming they have achieved among themselves a new consensus), or else they become deviant; in that case the sect, which is by our definition characterized by consensus, can deal with the situation only by rejecting the deviants. It is of the nature of a sect that it cannot make provision for deviance within its own internal structure.

Consensus and the Social System

It is in this respect that the sect as the pure type of religious system differs significantly from a 'social system' (assuming one accepts the validity of the concept of a social system). While a religious system requires a large measure of consensus in order to maintain itself and not disintegrate, social systems can and do cope success-fully with a certain degree of deviance, and even of internal conflict. One of the major criticisms of Talcott Parsons's account of the social system is that Parsons regards consensus as normative to a system; any deviance that occurs is regarded by Parsons as coming from 'outside' the system. Critics of the conceptual model offered by Parsons have emphasized that it accounts only for a social system in a state of equilibrium, and that some degree of change is inevitable in any society; hence some degree of disequilibrium may also be regarded as normal in any social system. David Lockwood, for example, objects with regard to the Parsonian model that 'pressures making for deviance ... are regarded as being a matter for investi-gation in each empirical situation as it arises', and that Parsons has no place in his scheme for 'social processes ... which systematically make for deviance and social change'.[11] Lockwood argues that in a fully dynamic analysis of social structure not only the *norm*, by which the social system is integrated, but also the *substratum* must be taken into account. By the substratum he means 'the factual disposition of means in the situation of action which structures *Lebenschancen* and produces interests of a non-normative kind – that is, interests other than those which actors have in conforming with the normative definition of the situation.'[12] Similar criticism comes from I. L. Horowitz: 'To place conflict outside the frame-work of social structure, or to go beyond that and see conflict as necessarily destructive of the social organism, is to place a definite premium on social equilibrium ... Only when social function is narrowly defined as social equilibrium can a sociological theory of conflict be viewed as an overt or hidden menace to the social system'.[13] The view of a social system that these criticisms imply is one that sees it as containing within itself the potential for the arising of social conflict and deviance, and as possessing also within itself mechanisms for coping with conflict without being destroyed or disintegrating. Now it is precisely this characteristic that the sect, the simple form of religious system does *not* possess. Deviance, issuing in internal conflict cannot be contained within the structure of a sect; instead, fission occurs and a new sect is produced. This is a necessary consequence of the fact that the principle of cohesion in a sect is that of voluntary consensus. If, however, one encounters a religious organization that can and does contain deviance within its structure, then the inference must be that this organization is by nature nearer to a social system than a sect.

There are various ways of accounting for the fact that a social system can contain deviance and not be destroyed by it. Here we are concerned with only one possibility. What holds a system together is not necessarily, as Parsons's view implies, the consensus of all the members of the system concerning values and goals. The 'moral identities' among men, which Emerson believed to be the source of a government's power, may in fact, as C. Wright Mills points out, be created by a government in its own interest. Such 'moral identities' may 'rest on the fact that institutional rulers successfully monopolize, and even impose, their master-symbols'.[14]

The situation envisaged here is one that is not altogether remote from that of certain kinds of religious organizations. D. S. Margoliouth, in the opening paragraphs of his account of Islam, makes the very significant observation that the prophet Muhammad founded not only a religion but also a nation. Certainly, the Islamic *umma* of Medina had the characteristics of a state; it was as much a political as a religious organization. It was a state which was able to draw upon one of the most powerful emotions, namely religious devotion, in its defence and in its expansion. Once it began to expand, its principle of internal cohesion was only partly that of voluntary consensus; it consisted also to a considerable extent of the consensus imposed by the institutional rulers, first the Prophet himself and then the Caliphs; it thus ceased very early in its history to exhibit the characteristics of the sect, the simple religious system, and instead assumed those of a social system.

The concept of a religion that is also a nation has deep roots in the Near East, especially in Egypt and in Israel. It is seen in one of its most famous and most pregnant forms in the Davidic kingdom; Yahwistic religion with its notion of a chosen people here became assimilated to Near Eastern state religions with their royal capitals, and temple cults. It was here that the ideas hardened into a militant religious nationhood, the consequences of which are still with us, both in Judaism and in those religions that have taken over Jewish ideas. It is significant that the prime minister of Israel, reported by William Rees-Mogg, recently said that she did not believe that the state of Israel could survive without the Jewish religion. The two are seen as complementary to each other. 'In what they see as a war for survival ... this extraordinary and ancient belief that the Jews are especially chosen by God to be a light to the world, becomes more alive to them, because it has been the agency of their survival as a people'.[15]

The process by which the early Christian sect became the Christian empire of Rome, with consensus (imposed by its institutional rulers) becoming the principle of its cohesion, does not need to be recounted here. Judaism, the Roman Church, Islam, Zionism, and the national churches or state-religions of Europe are all alike examples of the religious organization that approximates in its structure to a social system. In some cases, or in some periods of their history, they have exhibited the characteristics of those societies described by C. Wright Mills where consensus is *imposed*, 'Societies in which a dominant set of institutions controls the total society and superimposed its values by violence and the threat of violence'. At the other extreme from the voluntary consensus of the sect, then, is the consensus of coercion; the consensus of Islam under the Ummayad and Abbasid caliphs, the consensus of the Roman Church under the Inquisition, and of the Church of England under Henry VIII. What such systems were intended to achieve in their religious aspect was complete consensus of belief in obedience to what institutional authority prescribed, and the maximum conformity in attitudes and conduct.

If the question is now asked, To which model does the concept 'Christianity' approximate more closely, the pluralism of reciprocally different sects, or the unity of the nation-religion, it is not difficult to see what answer has to be given. Historically, however, the name 'Christianity' has been made to straddle the whole range of nation-churches and sects. It stands, that is to say, for an uneasy compromise between the two types; plurality of sects, and nation-church.

An Alternative to Consensus Christianity

Wilfred Cantwell Smith, in his *The Meaning and End of Religion*, while suggesting 'that terms such as Christianity, Buddhism, and the like must be dropped, as clearly untenable once challenged', sees the reality of the religious situation in terms of two interacting factors, 'different in kind, both dynamic: an historical "cumulative tradition", and the personal faith of men and women' (p. 194). This pair of concepts, cumulative tradition and personal faith are offered, if I have understood him correctly, as likely to provide a more realistic insight into the structure of what is commonly called Christianity. It is at this point that I am inclined to think his scheme needs supplementing; one needs to know more about the structure of the vast *intervening* area of institutions and organizations that extends between the personal faith of the individual and the cumulative tradition. The term Christianity has been pressed into service to straddle this whole area, but it does so only uneasily, since it is more appropriate to one pattern of religious organization than to the other: to the nation-church with its ideal of consensus and conformity rather than to the pluralism of the sects.

In discussing a similar situation in connection with social structure, I. L. Horowitz suggests that there is a third possibility in addition to the two opposing concepts of consensus and conflict, namely co-operation. He distinguishes between consensus and co-operation as follows: first, 'Consensus stands for agreement internally, i.e., in terms of shared perspectives, agreements on the rules of association and action, a common set of norms and values. Co-operation for its part makes no demands on role uniformity but only upon procedural rules. Co-operation concerns the settlement of problems in terms which make possible the continuation of differences and even fundamental disagreements'; second, 'Consensus is agreement on the content of behavior, while co-operation necessitates agreement only on the form of behavior'; third, 'Co-operation concerns toleration of differences, while consensus demands abolition of these same differences. If a game theory analogy be preferred, the distinction between co-operation and consensus might be stated in the following terms: consensus programs the termination of the game by insisting on the principle of unity and unilateral victory, whereas co-operation is pluralistic because it programs the continuation of the game by maintaining and insisting upon the legitimacy of differences.'[16]

I have quoted Horowitz at some length because all this seems highly relevant to the present situation in 'Christianity'. The acceptance of differences *between* sectarian groups, the agreement to differ, has not been outstandingly a feature of Christian history. When, as at the present time, 'a better way' is being sought, the danger is that we should assume the only alternative to conflicting plurality to be a monolithic unity of the kind that results from years of patient labouring towards consensus – a process that has been described as 'doctrinal and ecclesiastical carpentry', that is, the process of deciding how we can cut bits off here and there in order to make two sides fit together. The mistake may be seen to lie in the assumption that the only alternative to a plurality of *conflicting* sects that is worth pursuing is the unity of consensus, manifested in the organic union of, for example, Methodism with Anglicanism, of both with the Roman Church, and so on. But this would, as everyone knows, be an unstable, probably short-lived, and never complete unification (sects *will* arise, whatever the architects of union decide). There is an alternative, and that is a plurality of *co-operating* sects. The fact that different sects can live together in tolerance of each other, prepared to examine each other's points of view and learn from each other, in Hindu India but not in Christian Europe, is no credit to the latter. But the present practice of Christian Europe in this respect is not required by the Christian gospel; for it is not required that there should be a monolithic organization exhibiting consensus and conformity. What the Christian gospel requires above all is charity.

The implication of the concept of consensus is that we are, one way or the other, *forced to agree*. The fact is that men do not, even Christian men, when it comes to religious matters; indeed, one might say, *especially* Christian men. Since this is so, consensus will have to be imposed, with the result that all the differing apprehensions of spiritual reality must each die a little, must be clamped down upon, to make consensus possible. That is one theory; that way lies organic church union and credal unity. The other view is implied in all that Horowitz says concerning *co-operation*. It is the way of dialectic, the readiness to go on listening to each other's views and observing each other's different ways of doing things, the refusal to assume that the truth our sect (or our monolithic church) sees is the truth, the whole truth, and nothing but the truth.

The closing of the ranks, the compulsory uniting in the face of some supposed common enemy, is the prelude to communalism. When one religious organization has cause to believe that it is threatened by another, then communalism is often the result – the aggressive, militant communalism that arose in British India in the nineteenth century, for example. Such attitudes are traditionally alien to Indian culture, which is more favourable to the tolerance of plurality. Only when the principle of the monolithic nation-religion invaded India was this traditional tolerance of plurality shaken. At some point in the Christian history of Europe the same principle of the coercive consensus was introduced, and charity was forgotten.

Conclusions

1. The present widespread habit of speaking in terms of a sup-

posed but fictitious unitary entity called Christianity in order to claim a large authority for what is frequently a small-scale point of view is both dishonest and historically discreditable.

2. What is more, the cultivation of this fiction could have serious consequences in sharpening religious communalism in the modern world. It does not matter, in this case, that the belief that there is a single entity called Christianity to which all Christians belong and all non-Christians do not is false; for, as it is frequently observed by sociologists, *beliefs are real in their consequences.*

3. The movement that seeks to promote the spirit of *co-operation* among the plurality of actual Christian religious groups is one that most realistically meets the needs of a human situation in which the arising of new religious groups can never be proscribed, however much religious authoritarianism may dislike the fact; for sects, too, are here to stay. The movement for fostering such co-operation to which I refer is (in its original intention and purpose, at least) the World Council of Churches.

4. The leaders of the same movement at its inception frequently declared that organic church union was not the objective of the World Council. In fact, the period during which the World Council has been in existence has seen a number of schemes for moving in the direction of religious consensus rather than co-operation, that is, in the direction of organic union. In view of the arguments advanced in this paper, organic church union is not a mark of Christian maturity, rather the reverse. Moreover, it is open to question whether it is practically profitable either. Organic union is likely, every time it happens, to alienate at least a sizeable minority of former adherents, quite justifiably and understandably. Moreover, it was the westerner's insistence that he belonged to a system (Christianity) that set him apart and made him superior to the adherents of 'Hinduism', 'Buddhism', and 'Islam' that originally helped to escalate religious communalism. Withdrawal from the use of and belief in this concept could, even at this late stage, help to take some of the steam out of religious communalism. There are, however, some religious propagandists in the west who are totally opposed to co-operation of any kind with 'other' (non-Christian) religions. The fiction that there is a set of shared attitudes called Christianity tends to provide a wider basis of support for such propagandists. So long as the fiction of 'Christianity' is maintained

there will be a danger that other Christians will be drawn into such non-co-operation who might not otherwise adopt such an attitude. The religious non-co-operators are in the nature of things not open to dialogue and persuasion regarding their position of prejudice. The most that can be done is to isolate the virus and prevent it from doing more harm than it has by making clear that the area of real identity among Christians is, in fact, limited in many ways and since it is so, no good purpose can be served by pretending it is not. The acknowledgement that the concept 'Christianity' has very little credibility would assist a more precise and realistic view of things. On the other hand, the modern stampede towards organic union is a movement that fosters religious totalitarian attitudes. It is itself supported by the fictional notion 'Christianity', and each new organic union further strengthens belief in the fiction. The circle around the boundary of 'Christianity' is drawn in more and more boldly; those 'outside' are thus more and more firmly excluded, and dialogue inhibited.

NOTES

1   *The Meaning and End of Religion*, ch. 2.

2   Thomas R. Metcalf, *The Aftermath of Revolt: India 1857-1870* (1965) p. 292.

3   Metcalf, *op. cit.*, p. 295.

4   cf. Lal Mani Joshi, *Brahmanism, Buddhism and Hinduism* (Buddhist Publication Society, Kandy, Ceylon, 1970).

5   Max Weber, *The Sociology of Religion* (1963) ch. 12.

6   Weber, *op. cit.*, p. 201.

7   Weber, *op. cit.*, p. 203.

8   Weber, *op. cit.*, p. 188.

9   J. C. Ghosh, *Bengali Literature* (1948) p. 24.

10 Charles Y. Glock and Rodney Stark, *Religion and Society in Tension* (1965), and *American Piety: The Nature of Religious Commitment* (1968).

11 'Some Remarks on "The Social System"', in N. J. Demerath and R. A. Pearson, *System, Change and Conflict* (1967) p. 283.

12 *Op. cit.*, p. 284.

13 I. L. Horowitz, 'Consensus, Conflict and Co-operation', in Demerath and Pearson, *op. cit.*, p. 269f.

14 C. Wright Mills, *The Sociological Imagination* (1959).

15 William Rees-Mogg, 'The faith and the army', *The Times* (London) 17.2.70, p. 9.

16 I. L. Horowitz, *op. cit.*, pp. 278ff.

TREVOR LING is Professor of Comparative Religion in the University of Manchester. Author of *A History of Religion East and West*; *Buddhism and the Mythology of Evil*; *Buddha, Marx and God*, etc.

The Goals of Inter-Religious Dialogue

ERIC J. SHARPE

The problem of the 'relationship' between Christianity and other religious traditions has in recent years once more become a primary focus of theological and philosophical enquiry.[1] There are a number of historical reasons why this should be so. Vastly increased personal contacts between Christians and non-Christians; improved travel and communications; the rise and fall of the western colonial enterprise; the 'renaissance' of the eastern religions – these are just some of the external factors that have led to this remarkable development in Christian thought. Added to these there are the internal factors, such as the widespread popular rejection of any and every authoritarian basis for religion (though this may in some cases be more apparent than real), and the insistent questioning both of the values of western intellectual culture and of the West's role over against the remainder of the world. The result has been the gradual emergence of a new type (or perhaps the re-emergence of an old type) of 'theology of encounter', notable both for its rejection for some, at least, of the attitudes of the past, and for its emphasis on 'dialogue' as the only mode of inter-religious encounter appropriate to the present age.

This, I am aware, constitutes an over-simplification of a vastly complex process, extending over the better part of the century and making use of attitudes and theories of much greater antiquity. Nevertheless it may provide us with a starting point, and an explanation, however inadequate, of why the *word* 'dialogue' should be so popular at present. Indeed, a major difficulty that has to be faced at the outset is that the word has become excessively popular. One suspects that in many cases it has degenerated into a cliché, and that some of those who use it do so less out of profound conviction than because it happens to be fashionable. It is now widely accepted that dialogue between believers is a 'Good Thing'. Exactly why this should be so is all too often left unexpressed. The literature of 'inter-religious dialogue' is already extensive, and

growing rapidly; but it is not always clear in what sense (or senses)
the word is being used, and what are the presuppositions that lie
behind it.

A further source of difficulty arises from the fact that although
dialogue (if it preserves anything of its original meaning of 'conversation') is a practical activity, it is possible to write about it
purely in terms of theory and principle. In the area of the meeting
of Christians and Hindus, for instance, there are no doubt a variety
of reasons why the Christian (or at any rate the western) scholar
should suppose that his inherited western understanding of Hinduism qualifies him to make statements about the mode of contact
between Christians and Hindus and the 'relationship' between
Christianity and Hinduism on the theoretical level. But those who
have actually lived in experimental contact with adherents of
another religious tradition tend to be suspicious of statements of
this order. Klaus Klostermaier writes of his encounter with the
Hindus of Vrandaban:

> Dialogue was not a mere talking about religion; that is very
> often pure babble, vanity, self-glorification. Nor was dialogue
> the 'comparative religion' of experts. The comparison of religions
> is interesting only so long as one has not understood what
> religion is really all about. One can only compare what lies on
> the surface – maya. The real dialogue takes place in an ultimate,
> personal depth; it does not have to be a talking about religion.
> But something does distinguish real dialogue: the challenge ...[2]

It may perhaps be objected that a statement of this kind is purely
subjective, or at least that it presupposes a dimension of personal
religious experience that cannot be expected to serve as a norm for
all inter-religious contacts. But the point is a serious one, and raises
the question whether in fact there are any criteria of dialogue other
than those supplied by, in this case, the Christian tradition.

Clearly, then, there are theoretical presuppositions which determine the form that dialogue takes in any given instance; but equally
clearly, dialogue is a practical exercise, a mode of experimental
contact between persons whose inmost convictions differ: 'Dialogue
means the reaching out of one person towards the other; it is the
opening up to the other and his point of view; it requires the
turning to the other, the *Vergegenwärtigung* of the other.'[3]

If this said all that needed to be said, then the only presupposition
of dialogue would be the recognition of, say, the Hindu as a human

being. But other statements reveal other presuppositions, and I propose now to examine some of these.

First of all, it may be noted that there is a tendency in some quarters to use the word 'dialogue' merely to denote the converse of an 'old attitude' on the part of Christians towards non-Christian religions. This old attitude is assumed to have been one of total rejection, reflecting both an unwarranted sense of superiority on the part of the Christian and a deplorable ignorance of the actual religious phenomena of the non-Christian world. Professor Wilfred Cantwell Smith, in his book *The Meaning and End of Religion*, writes that ' "Dialogue" between members of differing traditions is nowadays replacing polemics, debate, and monologue preaching of traditional missionary policy.'[4] If these words are directed at Christians (as one must assume that they are) then they might have been more happily chosen. I find it hard to equate the words 'monologue preaching of traditional missionary policy' with any concrete phenomenon in the history of Christian missions, while 'polemics' and 'debate' are by no means the same thing; but that is by the way. The point is that an old order is changing.

In fact the old order has been changing for far longer than many modern writers tend to imagine. It was never as universal, even in the nineteenth century, as we are sometimes led to believe. Certainly negative attitudes towards non-Christian religions were expressed, and continue to be expressed; but to suppose that because the Christian was persuaded of the theological inadequacy of some particular form of non-Christian belief he was therefore devoid of sympathy and respect for all its manifestations, is simply untrue. To speak only of the area of Christian-Hindu encounter, missionaries such as T. E. Slater, F. W. Kellett, William Miller, J. N. Farquhar, Bernard Lucas, C. F. Andrews, Nicol MacNicol, and A. G. Hogg – in all of whom the present-day 'dialogue' attitude was anticipated – had advocated an attitude of sympathy towards Hinduism in the late nineteenth and early twentieth centuries.[5] Indian Christians such as Brahmabandhav Upadyay, K. M. Banerjea, and Nehemiah Goreh belong to the same period, and showed similar concerns. Somewhat more recently, A. J. Appasamy, P. Chenchaiah, V. Chakkarai, and other Indian Christians have done sterling work in attempting to express the ethos of Christianity in terms of the Indian cultural heritage well before the Second World War.[6] It is sometimes forgotten that the Tambaram Conference of 1938 that saw the publication of Hendrik Kraemer's magisterial book *The Christian Message in a Non-Christian World*, with its emphasis on the radical discontinuity between religions and the Christian gospel, also gave rise to the symposium *Rethinking Christianity in India*, one of the great landmarks in the history of Indian Christian thought – and a book as far removed from 'monologue preaching' as one could wish.[7]

It is odd, in view of current interest in the subject, that there is widespread ignorance of the history of Christian attitudes to non-Christian religions. Many a superficial judgement might in fact be avoided if past work in the area were more accurately known. As it is, the temptation on the one hand to condemn outright everything that does not stem from the fairly recent past, and on the other to read back into the past the concerns of the present, is wellnigh irresistible. Would that it were not so: would that fewer of the Lord's people were prophets, and more of them historians. It might then be realized that talk of 'old' and 'new' attitudes is seldom other than misleading, since attitudes are usually determined less by temporal sequence (except among determined neophiliacs) than by theological conviction. It might also be recognized that 'dialogue' cannot be recommended just because it happens to be newer than some other attitude.

The attitude of controversy has of course not been superseded. It has been overlaid in some areas, undermined in others; but as long as there are Christians for whom the acceptance of one authority (usually in practice the authority of the Bible) inevitably means the rejection of all competing authorities, it will remain. I have written elsewhere of the stages by which this attitude came to be modified on the Protestant side of the Christian-Hindu encounter in India, with the emergence of 'comparative religion' in the West, and the gradual acceptance of certain of its presuppositions – notably that of sympathy with all local manifestations of universal 'religion' – by members of the Christian missionary corps.[8] Parallel with this development it came to be realized (though not for the first time) that if Christianity were ever to become a genuinely Indian form of religion, it would have to find genuinely Indian forms of expression, and that these could never emerge without close and appreciative study of the Indian cultural heritage, and the modification of western Christian intellectual ideas into forms better suited to the Indian mind. 'Educated India,' wrote the Scottish missionary A. G. Hogg in 1905, 'declares that she will never become Christian; and certainly she will never definitely embrace Christianity until Christian doctrines have been recast in a less alien mould.'⁹

To this end gifted and devoted scholars sought to immerse them-selves in all things Indian, to cease to indulge in barren polemics, to speak accurately and sympathetically of Indian religion, while nevertheless maintaining their faithfulness to the Christian revel-ation as they understood it. Facile solutions to complex problems were avoided far more assiduously – and successfully – than modern writers, with all the wisdom of hindsight, find it easy to credit. Of course times have changed; of course their work has been partly superseded. But without it, in India at least, what we now know as 'the Christian-Hindu dialogue' would never have come about.

Building on these foundations, the great age of dialogue began in the years immediately after the Second World War. Incidentally, one of its first concerns was to find a way out of the impasse in which the dominance of Hendrik Kraemer's theology seemed to have left the theology of encounter in 1938. In India, its early development was associated above all with such outstanding names as P. D. Devanandan and D. G. Moses,¹⁰ and more recently with the leaders of the Christian Institute for the Study of Religion and Society in Bangalore, notably Herbert Jai Singh and M. M. Thomas.¹¹ However, the last decade has seen the spectacular emergence of Roman Catholic theology, liberated by Vatican II, into the forefront of the debate. J. A. Cuttat, H. le Saux (Swami Abhishiktānanda), Raymond Panikkar, and Klaus Klostermaier have all made important contributions.¹²

As a result of these intensive studies and practical initiatives, it is now possible to see a little more clearly the variety of pre-suppositions that in fact underly this single word 'dialogue'. Shared by all is the assumption of common ground between believers. But the nature and extent of that common ground is disputed. So, too, is the precise objective, or goal, which it is hoped that the activity of dialogue will achieve. The dialogue may be motivated as ex-pressing a shared quest for intellectual clarity and understanding; a shared humanity; a shared involvement in a particular secular situation; or a shared relationship to ultimate reality, or God. Accordingly I propose to distinguish between four types of object-ive which may motivate the practice of dialogue. These I shall call, for the sake of convenience, (a) Discursive Dialogue, (b) Human Dialogue, (c) Secular Dialogue and (d) Interior Dialogue. It must be emphasized, however, that in any given situation of encounter it will seldom (perhaps never) be possible to say that any one goal is being aimed at separately from the other three; all four may in fact be involved simultaneously. It goes without saying, too, that believers may reject out of hand the notion that there is in fact common ground between themselves and adherents of other religious traditions – in which case to speak of dialogue is neither necessary nor desirable.

In what follows, I draw my illustrations entirely from the field of the encounter between Christian and Hindu traditions in India.

Discursive Dialogue

For those who assume that the human reason is competent to lead individuals into an understanding of truth, the activity previously called 'dialectic' or 'debate', when transmuted into dialogical terms, may be characterized as 'discursive dialogue'. It involves meeting, listening and discussion on the level of mutual competent intellectual inquiry. Sympathy and respect for the other person's position are absolutely essential; so, too, are accurate knowledge of one's own religious tradition and scrupulous honesty in expressing its content. If an attempt be made to misrepresent or conceal, or if there should be failure to listen to, or trust, what the partner in dialogue is saying, then nothing can be achieved. Nor is very much likely to be achieved if the partners are unequally matched (though presumably the acquisition of information is possible whatever the conditions.)

I do not, however, propose to discuss this particular mode of dialogue in detail in this context. Sympathetic encounter between believers must, it seems to me, inevitably begin on this level; and there is a long history of inter-religious encounter in which its conditions have been amply met. Wherever there has been open, courteous discussion between Christians and non-Christians on matters having to do with faith or beliefs, one might say that there has been discursive dialogue (if, that is, one insists on using the word 'dialogue'). It has grown out of intellectual curiosity and intellectual conviction, and has ideally aimed at laying bare the convictions, doctrines and dogmas that form the staple of separate religious traditions. When undertaken by Christians, such discussion has frequently led to the passing of Christian theological judgements on the non-Christian material – a procedure that is at least defensible, and may be inevitable, as John Baillie pointed out in his book *The Interpretation of Religion*:

> But religious judgements being what they are ... it is psychologically an impossible feat, as well as logically a self-contradictory desire, *not* to make one's own fundamental religious convictions the criterion of religious truth. If we believe them to be true (as we must do, if they are really convictions), then we are, *ipso facto*, making them the criterion. And, once again, what *other* criterion is at all conceivable?[13]

Baillie wrote this in 1928, since when the climate of theological opinion has changed radically. It is now widely held that 'beliefs' and intellectual conceptualizations (on which discursive dialogue depends) are of little or no ultimate value, especially in the area of inter-religious encounter. Accordingly, other modes of dialogue attempt to pass beyond encounter on the level of reasoned discourse to different levels of common ground – common humanity, common involvement in a secular situation, and a common quest for reality respectively.

Human Dialogue

Doctrines divide; humanity unites. Put in its simplest form, this is the conviction (a rational conviction) that underlies the greater part of the activity that is today called inter-religious dialogue. The 'I-thou' relationship is all-important; what is said or done is less so.[14] The only *Anknüpfungspunkt* that matters is that of common humanity, and therefore it is essential to penetrate divisive doctrinal and ideological rationalizations in order to get at the root of the matter – the fact that man is meeting man.

Since this mode of dialogue has its roots in a philosophy of a broadly existentialist character, there are no *a priori* reasons why it should be interpreted in theological terms (though equally the influence of existentialism and phenomenology in Christian circles makes such an interpretation quite feasible). The linking of 'human' and theological categories is seen clearly in this typical statement by C. Murray Rogers:

> This dialogue between Christian and Hindu in which a number of us find ourselves involved has, as an essential precondition, a willingness and a readiness to listen to the other *as other*. We may not listen in order to prepare our next words of approach, proclamation or attack, but with the awareness that Christ speaks

to us from the other. Far from expecting to despise or belittle what we hear we will be set to appreciate. To listen means therefore far more than simply to stop talking; it demands a silence in oneself *in order to understand the non-Christian brother as he understands himself'* (my italics), 'a "putting into brackets" ' of my own explicit Christian convictions. The moment will come in real dialogue when the Christian will speak and when that comes it will not be a prefabricated answer but a word to a partner who has been understood.[15]

Substantially the same point is made by Wilfred Cantwell Smith, in his book *Questions of Religious Truth*:

> ... true religion is a relation between man and man: a living relation; an actual relation, new every morning, among particular, real men in concrete, changing situations. We *believe*, as Christians, that our neighbor is a person, a child of God, and that we ought to love him; but our *knowing* that he is (as distinct from believing it) and our loving him (as distinct from feeling that we ought to love him), are questions of how Christian (adjectivally) we really are, so as to see him as a person rather than being distracted into thinking of him as a Muslim or a Buddhist or a Jew – and thus seeing, not him as he personally is, but an image of him that has been abstractly constructed.[16]

The value of an attitude such as this in creating the conditions on which sympathetic encounter can take place need scarcely be stressed. But like all idealistic attitudes, it has its weaknesses. For instance, if it should be tacitly held that precisely formulated religious beliefs are of relatively little value in comparison with the 'person' who holds them (which seems often to be the case), then not only will there be difficulty in appreciating the precise nature of those beliefs, but there may also be a tendency to treat the 'partner in dialogue' as an abstraction, separable from his cultural, intellectual and religious setting. Further, this approach as a whole may degenerate into romanticism, and fail to do what it specifically sets out to do, i.e. to bring persons face to face, by ignoring the mind as a constituent element of human personality. It is all very well to say that it is more important for the Christian to meet the Hindu as a man than to meet the man as a Hindu; but the man *is* a Hindu, and possesses (if this is the right word) a 'Hindu mind', which needs to be understood intellectually, as well as perceived intuitively. Intellectual problems in the area of religion, if shelved and bypassed, have a way of returning, as the Christian ecumenist knows only too well. Thus to speak of dialogue in purely 'human' categories seems to me to be dangerous without further definition.

Secular Dialogue

It is a short step from 'human dialogue' to that type of encounter that concentrates entirely on the situation of man in the world, aiming solely at the recognition of joint concern and the need for joint secular action, irrespective of divergencies in religious conviction. In the Christian theological setting, the emergence of theories of this kind has been facilitated by the vogue of secular theologies or pseudo-theologies, the categories of which have increasingly of late been used in the situation of Christian-Hindu encounter.

In an essay in the volume *Inter-Religious Dialogue*, called 'Preparation for Dialogue', Herbert Jai Singh (the editor of the volume) points out that in every religious faith there is 'a growing interest in the life of this world', and that religious renewal 'expresses itself primarily in good works geared to the redemption of all forms of life here and now'.[17] This has meant in practice that all the great religions have shown increased interest in social and political action for the amelioration of man's lot on earth; this in turn has set the stage for inter-religious dialogue. From the Christian point of view, the acceptance of that mode of thought broadly called 'scientific' and the notion of 'desacralization' are of the utmost importance in this setting. Jai Singh writes:

> As long as men were enslaved to sacred books, sacred custom and sacred hierarchies of religious leadership, discussion was restricted to very narrow limits. The process of desacralization has lifted the heavy weight of these burdens and left men free to talk about realities which pave the way for the future advancement of man. Desacralization turns the eyes of men to the world, to time and history, and the realities of history are often more manageable for purposes of dialogue than the supra-mundane things of an ethereal world.[18]

Indeed they are more 'manageable': and if a Hindu and a Christian can talk together about the details of life together in the same

Indian community, bypassing the things on which they do not agree, then this is, in one sense, dialogue:

> When intellectuals of different faiths discuss religions, they often assume the good of man as the final criterion of truth. This emphasis on man changes the whole context of dialogue. Men are naturally drawn into discussion, not so much as Hindus, Christians and Muslims, but as men engaged in the common struggle of humanity for food, dignity, and justice – as men involved in a common destiny of bearing the burdens and responsibilities of common living. This clears the air for dialogue ... It is the discussion of actual concrete problems that brings into focus underlying fundamental traditional beliefs.[19]

It is clear from the last sentence that in Jai Singh's view, 'secular dialogue' is more a matter of emphasis than of exclusive concern. However, elsewhere in the same volume articles by the Dane Kaj Baagø and the American Richard Taylor make more sweeping claims. Baagø in particular asserts that the Christian must be free and flexible in his contacts with other religions, and that this state can be achieved only by the process of secularization, which will remove traditional doctrinal, organizational, and hierarchical hindrances to close contact. He concludes that '... the true dialogue with men of other faiths can best be established by those who have left the organized church or stay outside it'.[20] Taylor approaches the problem from a different angle, but ends by stating that 'Increasingly our dialogue must be not so much with religions as with the world ... Usually this will not be a church-world dialogue, but a dialogue of men of various faiths on the pressing social issues, and toward their solution.'[21]

Now while one would not wish to argue that secular concerns can have no place within the framework of inter-religious encounter, clearly much depends on the theological presuppositions with which this area is approached. If the 'true' focus of religious concern is seen as being the situation of man in the world, and if God is regarded as wholly immanent (a stance of faith for which some would argue), then the secular conclusion is inevitable. In fact, though, these conclusions are not universally drawn, either by Hindus or by Christians; and where they are not, the suspicion may be felt either that 'secular dialogue' is a matter of expediency, or that even if secular concern is legitimate, it can never be more than a face of encounter.[22] As with 'human dialogue', if elevated

into an absolute principle, it may lead to the avoidance of fundamental issues. Although the secular Christian and the Vedāntin
may have to live in the same world, it is *a priori* unlikely that their
respective interpretations of the world in which they live will have
a great deal in common; and to dismiss the interpretation (on which
action must be based) as an irrelevancy seems to me to be utterly
irresponsible. Presumably this seldom happens; but the danger
has to be recognized and guarded against.

Interior Dialogue

The fourth mode of dialogue that I believe can be distinguished
in contemporary debate owes little either to the intellectual or the
existential tradition in recent Christian history, although it may
make selective use of both. Its *locus* is the mystical, contemplative
tradition, and its advocates are normally those trained in that
tradition. A basic (though not always acknowledged) assumption
is that all intellectualization, doctrinal or otherwise, is of limited
relevance, useful only as a means of approach to the divine mystery.

One of the most outstanding representatives of this approach in
India today is Fr. H. le Saux (Swami Abhishiktānanda). He writes
that

> The first condition of a fruitful dialogue of salvation (the
> equivalent of my term 'interior dialogue') with our non-Christian
> brothers and especially with Hindus is ... to acquire an adequate
> knowledge of the traditional culture of India and of her religion
> and spirituality.[23]

But he maintains equally that the dialogue cannot proceed very
far on this intellectual basis, since '... the most essential qualification
for a fruitful inter-religious dialogue is not so much an acute mind,
as a contemplative disposition of the soul'.[24] Elsewhere he states
the same principle still more forcefully:

> It is only on the contemplative level that any proper religious
> dialogue can be engaged in with Hindus; but Hindus will never
> let themselves become involved in such a dialogue until they
> know for sure that their interlocutor is aware at least of the
> interiority which has been revealed to them by their own spiritual
> Masters. We may even say boldly that lack of intellectual prep-
> aration may be to a great extent at least made up for by con-

templative insight, whereas no amount of learning is able to make up for the lack of contemplative spirit.[25]

Other expressions of this same conviction are not hard to find. For instance, Dom Bede Griffiths uncovers a basic theological presupposition when he writes:

> What is required is a meeting of the different religious traditions at the deepest level of their experience of God. Hinduism is based on a deep mystical experience and everywhere seeks not simply to know 'about' God, but to 'know God', that is to experience the reality of God in the depths of the soul. It is at this level that Christian and Hindu have to meet ...[26]

And he considers that this meeting can best take place within the setting of the contemplative life, 'in which contact can be made with the Hindu mystical tradition'.[27]

Finally I may cite part of the statement made by the 1969 Bombay Consultation on the Theology of Hindu-Christian Dialogue (in which I was privileged to take part), in which it was suggested that

> ... we would do well to pay far greater attention than we are wont to pay to negative theology, in which formulations remain flexible ... Negative Theology is closely related to the awareness of God's awesome greatness. *It is more a spiritual discipline than an intellectual exercise* [my italics]. It negates the primacy of logic and conceptual knowledge and relies on experiences, intuition and contemplation. It agrees with the unique character of advaitic experience ...[28]

The concern of interior dialogue is clearly not that of either human dialogue or secular dialogue, and it makes use of the categories of discursive dialogue only as a transitional stage, to be left behind as soon as may be possible. It presupposes that God reveals himself in every religious tradition, and that the essence of religion is to be found in the mystical experience of oneness with the divine. For this reason, Christian contemplatives tend to speak in the warmest and most appreciative terms of the corresponding tradition within Hinduism, that of Advaita Vedānta, and to find spiritual sustenance from the Upanishads and the Bhagavad-Gītā just as much as from the Bible. Nevertheless the tendency is to interpret every mystical experience in Christian theological terms, for instance by speaking (as Fr. Pannikar has done) of 'the unknown

Christ of Hinduism'.[29] Much might be said of this, but it will perhaps be sufficient to cite as an example this passage from a Christian prayer for Indian Independence Day, produced by Indian theological students:

> Lord Jesus Christ, help us discover your hidden presence in the living traditions of our country, so that we too may be led by this discovery from the unreality of our narrow views to the Reality of your infinite Presence; from the darkness of our ignorance of your ways to the light of your full Revelation; and from the death of our sinful self-sufficiency to the Immortal Life of your love:
>
> *Asato mā sad gamaya! tamaso mā jyotir gamaya! mṛtyor māmṛtaṁ gamaya!*[30]

The most pressing question that is raised by this particular mode of dialogue concerns less the area of contact between Christian and Hindu than the diversity of traditions with Christianity, particularly since the claim is made that 'proper' religious dialogue with Hindus can be undertaken 'only on the contemplative level'. Unfortunately for this claim, all Christians are not contemplative; nor is there any overwhelming justification for the assumption that Christianity as such is to be measured by contemplative standards. True, there are spiritual traditions *within* Christianity and Hinduism that are motivated by similar concerns; but in neither case can the tradition in question be held up as normative – at least, not without arousing opposition. The contemplative tradition is no more normative for Christianity than the tradition of Advaita Vedānta for Hinduism; each is but a facet of a complex whole. Therefore to speak of interior dialogue as the *only* viable form of communication between Christians and Hindus is acceptable only within these particular traditions, while the evangelical Christian, for instance, may feel that there are important questions of principle that are dangerously obscured.

From this brief review it may perhaps be seen that the goal or goals of inter-religious dialogue are as varied as the modes of dialogue that I have tried to describe. In only one case is there a fair measure of clarity. The goal of discursive dialogue is usually taken to be a better understanding of the other person's religious stance, possibly in order to facilitate the communication of the Christian message. It has been repeatedly pointed out this century that it is useless for the Christian missionary to embark upon a

programme of evangelization without a thorough prior knowledge
of the people to whom his message is addressed – their language,
their culture, their modes of thought, religious and secular, and
so on.[31] And for those whose Christian faith involves an imperative
missionary dimension, and who are still prepared to make use of the
terminology of dialogue, the attempt to enter into a sympathetic
understanding of the non-Christian must take some such form as
that which I have called discursive dialogue.

But whether or not there should be this 'orthodox' motivation,
it is difficult to conceive of practical inter-religious contact utterly
divorced from the discursive, intellectual element. Even in interior
dialogue, which by definition transcends the limits of reason, a
beginning has to be made somewhere, with the acquisition of
adequate knowledge.[32] The goal is, however, the intuitive recognition of a shared experience of the transcendent reality. Similarly
with human and secular dialogue: without recognition of the
categories in which men express their human and secular concerns,
it is difficult to imagine any progress whatsoever being made.

It is, however, fair to ask, Progress towards what? Unity, certainly, or at least improved communication in that intermediate
stage between manifest disunity and future unity into which many
feel that we have now entered. In such cases it is by no means clear
whether the unity envisaged is organizational, federal, or 'spiritual'.
Suffice it to say that most of the advocates of dialogue at present
see this activity as a necessary contribution to the spiritual well-
being of mankind. Parallels may be drawn with the experience of
the Christian churches in the ecumenical era, but these are seldom
other than misleading.

In the Indian situation, dialogue frequently aims, from the
Christian side, not so much at future unity (unless this be conceived
of in eschatological terms) as at the more immediate goal of the
indigenization of Indian Christian thought. Perhaps the most potent
motivation here is the negative one of the rejection of past cultural
intolerances. The Christian, it is said (or rather implied) ought to
engage in intensive dialogue with the Hindu in order to learn to
express his faith in Indian (i.e.. Hindu) terms. The replacement, or
at any rate the supplementing, of the Old Testament by the
Upanishads as the Indian *praeparatio evangelica* has frequently
been mooted for precisely these reasons, and is now being increasingly accepted, as is Christian worship in which use is made of
'baptized' Hindu symbols. Theologically speaking, the assumption –

that God has spoken, and is speaking, in the Hindu tradition – is not a new one, but it is today accepted by almost all Christians. In a recent, and extreme, form the Hindu may be regarded as an 'anonymous Christian', but speculations of this order have little practical value outside the Christian theological circles in which they originated.[33]

I began by saying that dialogue is necessarily a practical activity. Perhaps this same idea could be equally well expressed by saying that adherents of different religious traditions must meet, and ought to meet, seriously and sympathetically, both in order to find out in what they agree and in what they differ. This being so, it is illuminating to observe the variety of presuppositions that underlie the use of the word 'dialogue'. Clearly the mere act of adopting a popular word does not ensure agreement as to its precise meaning. One is sometimes almost forced to reflect that the cause of sympathetic inter-religious dialogue might be better served if the word were to be laid aside for a time. I agree with Richard Taylor that there is a potential conflict in principles between discursive and human (or 'Buberian') dialogue, though I do not agree that the achievement of discursive dialogue only is necessarily a 'crippling situation'.[34] But when a single word can be used in such diverse senses, and serve the interests of attitudes involving distinctively different presuppositions (rational and non-rational), clearly some semantic tidying up is necessary. Ultimately the point at issue may be whether, in Taylor's words, 'intellectualizing in terms of categories becomes a putting up of thought processes as a screen between man and man',[35] or whether those same thought processes are, in the religious sense, our only key to the understanding of what men actually believe – as opposed to what we would like them to believe.

This has being a very brief, and necessarily superficial, review of some of the ways in which the term 'dialogue' is currently being used in the situation of Christian-Hindu encounter. We have seen that the word conceals a variety of presuppositions and attitudes, depending on widely divergent theological and practical concerns. Dialogue does certainly involve first and foremost from the Christian side the rejection of the impatience and polemics and partisan controversies of the past – largely because the Christian theological foundations on which these once rested have now been widely revised. Once this point has been passed, and once it has been accepted that there is common ground between believers, dialogue may turn in any one of a number of directions – intellectual, personal, secular, or contemplative. Its advocates almost all assume, however, that the causes of past intolerance have to do with the doctrinal and other constructions that men have built around their central religious commitment, and seek for areas of common concern in which those constructions are transcended, penetrated, or avoided. But before these objectives can be achieved, it seems to me that there must be a much greater measure of clarity concerning the meaning of dialogue. As yet nothing approaching a consensus has emerged. If this paper has served at least to demonstrate something of the nature of the ground to be covered, its purpose will have been achieved.

NOTES

1   The literature is already extensive. Among recent books of a more general type may be mentioned: E. C. Dewick, *The Christian Attitude to Other Religions* (Cambridge, 1953); H. Kraemer, *Religion and the Christian Faith* (London, 1956); E. L. Allen, *Christianity among the Religions* (London, 1960); A. J. Boyd, *Christian Encounter* (Edinburgh, 1961); C. G. Diehl, *Kristendomens möte med religionerna* (Lund, 1961); S. C. Neill, *Christian Faith and Other Faiths* (London, 1961); P. Tillich, *Christianity and the Encounter of the World Religions* (New York, 1963); C. F. Hallencreutz, *New Approaches to Men of Other Faiths* (Geneva, 1970).

2   K. Klostermaier, *Hindu and Christian in Vrindaban* (E. T. London, 1969), p. 102.

3   P. Schreiner, in *Journal of Ecumenical Studies* (1969), p. 394.

4   W. Cantwell Smith, *The Meaning and End of Religion* (Mentor ed., New York, 1964), p. 177.

5   E. J. Sharpe, *Not to Destroy but to Fulfil* (Lund, 1965), *passim*.

6   K. Baagø, *Pioneers of Indigenous Christianity* (Bangalore & Madras, 1969), *passim.*, R. H. S. Boyd, *An Introduction to Indian Christian Theology* (Madras, 1969), *passim.*

7   G. V. Job and others, *Rethinking Christianity in India* (Madras, 1938). Cf. D. A. Thangasamy, *The Theology of Chenchiah* (Bangalore, 1966), P. T. Thomas, *The Theology of Chakkarai* (Bangalore, 1968).

8   Sharpe, *op. cit.*, pp. 35ff.

9   A. G. Hogg, *Karma and Redemption* (Madras, 1909), p. 103. The

words quoted were originally written in an article in the *Madras Christian College Magazine* for 1905, and later reprinted.

10 See e.g. P. D. Devanandan, *Preparation for Dialogue* (Bangalore, 1964); M. M. Thomas, 'The Significance of the Thought of Paul D. Devanandan for a Theology of Dialogue', in H. Jai Singh (ed.), *Inter-Religious Dialogue* (Bangalore, 1967), pp. 1-37; D. G. Moses, *Religious Truth and the Relation between Religions* (Madras, 1950).

11 See e.g. H. Jai Singh (ed.), *Inter-Religious Dialogue* (Bangalore, 1967); M. M. Thomas, *The Christian Response to the Asian Revolution* (London, 1966); *The Acknowledged Christ of the Indian Renaissance* (London, 1969, Bangalore & Madras, 1970); and various issues of the CISRS journal, *Religion and Society*.

12 See e.g. H. le Saux, *La recontre de l'hindouisme et du christianisme* (Paris, 1966); E. T. *Hindu-Christian Meeting Point*, (Bombay & Bangalore, 1969); *The Church in India* (Madras, 1969); R. Panikkar, *The Unknown Christ of Hinduism* (London, 1964); K. Klostermaier, *Kristvidyā* (Bangalore, 1967); *Hindu and Christian in Vrindaban* (London, 1969).

13 J. Ballie, *The Interpretation of Religion* (repr. Nashville, 1956), p. 123. The identical point is made by Leslie Newbigin, *The Finality of Christ* (London, 1969), p. 20: 'If religion deals with men's ultimate commitments, then it is surely wise to recognize that a religious man does not have a point of view which transcends that commitment and which enables him to judge other religious commitments impartially.'

14 For this reason it is sometimes called 'Buberian dialogue'. See R. W. Taylor's 'The Meaning of Dialogue', in H. Jai Singh, *op. cit.*, p. 56. I must acknowledge at this point that I am indebted in my classification of modes of dialogue to Taylor's article, though my conclusions differ somewhat from his.

15 *Religion and Society* (March 1965), p. 39.

16 W. Cantwell Smith, *Questions of Religious Truth* (London, 1967), p. 115f.

17 Jai Singh, *op. cit.*, p. 42f.

18 *Ibid.*, p. 47.

19 *Ibid.*, p. 48f.

20 K. Baagø, 'Dialogue in a Secular Age', in Jai Singh, *op cit.*, p. 140.

21 R. W. Taylor, *op. cit.*, p. 64.

22 Newbigin, *op. cit.*, p. 63: 'Rightly understood, the process of secularization is an extending of the area of freedom wherein man

has the opportunity to understand and respond to what God has done for the world in Jesus Christ.'

23   Abhishiktananda, *The Church in India* (Madras, 1969), p. 33.

24   Idem., 'The Way of Dialogue', in Jai Singh, *op. cit.*, p. 85.

25   *The Church in India*, p. 41f.

26   Griffiths, *Christ in India* (New York, 1967), p. 46f.

27   *Ibid.*, p. 65.

28   The entire report of this Consultation will be found in *Religion and Society* (June 1969), pp. 69ff. The quotation is from p. 80.

29   R. Panikkar, *The Unknown Christ of Hinduism* (London, 1964), p. 35: 'The relationship between Hinduism and Christianity, finds in the linking conjunction "and" a more or less adequate expression, but this "and" does not express relationships such as falsehood-truth, darkness-light, sin-sanctity, damnation-salvation and similar pairs. One tends more to associate it with such pairs as potency-act, seed-fruit, forerunner-real presence, symbol-reality, desire-accomplishment, allegory-thing-in-itself, and so on; or ... there is a certain relationship belonging to the Christian dynamism of death and resurrection.'

30   *The Living Spring* (August 1968), pp. 14ff. The Sanskrit text is from the Brihadāraṇyaka Upanishad (I.iii.28): 'From the unreal lead me to the real! From darkness lead me to the light! From death lead me to immortality!'

31   See Sharpe, *Not to Destroy but to Fulfil*, pp. 206ff.

32   'The first requisite for tolerance, as well as for intransigence, is mutual knowledge' (Panikkar, *op. cit.*, p. 33). My colleague David Young, commenting on the first draft of this paper, wrote at this point: 'I would say that interior dialogue requires a great deal of preparation in which concepts and words and discursive thought will play their part. But my main point is that if contemplation is to be termed a form of dialogue, it must be shot through and through with the sense of personal encounter, the sense that this activity is meaningful because it is done in the presence of others and because it leads one to know and understand others more fully.'

33   The clearest statement of this position is in E. Hillman, *The Wider Ecumenism: Anonymous Christianity and the Church* (London, 1968); see also J. Neuner (ed.) *Christian Revelation and World Religions* (London, 1967).

34   R. W. Taylor, *op. cit.*, p. 57.

35   *Ibid.*

ERIC SHARPE is Lecturer in Religious Studies in the University of Lancaster, and author of *Not to Destroy but to Fulfil* and a number of articles.

The Misunderstanding of Hinduism

SANTOSH CHANDRA SENGUPTA

Despite the present climate of dialogue between the different faiths, the understanding of other religions is often motivated and biased, and has resulted in grave misrepresentations. What appears to be a dialogue between faiths is often only a monologue. Further, the bias appears even among some experts in religions. Some of the Barthians still believe that 'The God of Muhammad is an idol among other idols'. Emil Brunner contrasts general revelation with the special revelation given by 'the God of the Bible'. Some of the Hindu Pundits treat the Bhagavad-Gītā as if it were the only spiritual scripture. Some Islamic writers consider Muhammad superior to any other prophet or any other religion. It is good that responsible scholars in comparative religion have raised their voices against this unfortunate situation and have expressed the need for an objective understanding of other religions. They have also rightly pointed out that one cannot have the correct perspective on a religion when it is viewed as an abstraction. It must be studied as the living faith of practising believers. Thus Huston Smith opens his work on the religions of man with a picture of men at prayer in different lands and varying traditions. For the prayer-situation is typical of that which is most alive in the living faiths of men. It is important to note that the study of religions as living faiths provides an insight into the essential connectedness or the unity of the different religions, to which I shall refer presently. Broadly speaking, the wrong approach in the understanding of religions has its source in two factors: (a) a want of sympathy for other religions and (b) the scientific bias towards abstraction. It is this approach that has led to the misunderstanding of religions. As an example, I shall inquire into the nature of the misunderstanding of Hinduism.

In the West, Hinduism has been generally represented as the religion of abstractness and negation. Thus, many western scholars describe Hinduism in negatives in order to contrast it with Christianity. The familiar language of the contrast is that Hinduism is other-worldly or world and existence-negating, mystical or monistic (of the abstract or absolutistic type) and transethical (which amounts to the negation of the ethical sphere), while the Christian religion is this-worldly or world and existence-affirming, theistic and ethical. This standard western description of Hinduism is partly due to some of the Indian scholars' one-sided approach to Hindu philosophy and religion. They select one of the systems of Hinduism for which they have a preference and interpret the whole of Hindu thought in the light of that system. The system in this case is Advaita-Vedānta (pure monism) as expounded by Śaṅkara. However, the interpretation of Hinduism as the religion of abstraction and negation amounts to a radical misrepresentation of the nature or essence of Hindu religion. I shall try to show that Hinduism is not what it is often characterized as being, and that it cannot be contrasted with Christianity in the manner referred to. Those who characterize Hinduism in negatives mainly refer to the Hindu views of ultimate reality, the world, and human existence, and liberation. It is contended that in the Hindu view (a) the ultimate reality is an indeterminate and impersonal identity, an identity that excludes difference; (b) the world is devoid of significance and is unreal; and (c) liberation consists in transcendence of the ethical sphere and in renunciation of the world. I shall examine each of these ideas.

The Hindu View of Ultimate Reality

The interpreters who characterize the Hindu view of ultimate reality as pure monism or as pantheism appeal to one or two hymns of the Ṛgveda, the negative passages of the Upanishads, and the acosmism of Śaṅkara-Vedānta. My contention is that a closer study of the Vedas and the Upanishads and the consideration of the Bhagavad-Gītā (which has a much greater influence on most Hindus than the Vedānta), indicates that the dominant Hindu conception of God has an essentially theistic character that is similar in certain respects to that found in Christian theism. There is no denying that one or two hymns of the Ṛgveda, which is one of the many Vedas, point to the impersonal and indeterminate nature of the ultimate. But against these one or two hymns there are four other hymns that refer to the notion of the ultimate or God as Viśvakarma, i.e. the maker and the lord of the universe. We know that the Vedic conception of God evolved from polytheism to monotheism via what is known as henotheism. The monotheistic conception of God as the creator and lord of the world is essentially different from the abstract and pantheistic notion. In the Yajurveda, God is addressed as Pita, Father. 'Salutations to Thee, our Father, Awaken us and cause us no harm.' To come to the Upanishads: there is no denying that there are negative passages here, passages that deny personality and qualities to the ultimate. One typical passage is 'This is the imperishable, O Gārgī, wise people adore – not gross, not subtle, not short, not long – without darkness, without air, without space, without taste, without smell ... without mind, without light, without breath, without form and without inside and outside' (Brihad, 3.8.8). However against a few such passages there are numerous passages that affirm the ultimate as a person having qualities. To quote: 'Vedāhametaṁ Purushaṁ Mahāntana' (Śvet, 3.8) ('I have known who is the Supreme Person'); 'Taṁ Vedyaṁ Purushaṁ Veda Yathā Ma Vo Mṛtyuḥ Parivyathāḥ' (Praśna, 6.6). ('Know him the Person who only is to be known so that death may not grieve thee'). Now the question arises: how can one reconcile the two types of passages, one that denies personality to the ultimate and the other that admits the ulti- mate as a person? One view is that a reconciliation is possible if we view the different passages from two standpoints – the transcendental and the phenomenal: It is from the phenomenal and not the transcendental standpoint that we can admit the deter- minateness and the personality of the supreme reality. However, this attempt at reconciliation is not tenable, for the two standpoints cannot be related or reconciled, since they belong to the spheres of knowledge and ignorance respectively, spheres that exclude each other.

The correct view of the matter is that there is no real problem of reconciliation between the two types of passages, for the difference between the two is essentially one of emphasis. In the stress on the transcendence of the ultimate the negative passages occur, while in the emphasis on the immanence of the ultimate the other type of passage occurs. Besides, if we study the negative passages closely we find that many of the predicates denied in the negative statements belong to the level of finitude. That is, what is denied of God, the ultimate, is that which limits His infinitude and unlimitedness. It is patent that this negation is essential to the affirmation of religion. The common upanishadic view is that the Supreme Reality is both impersonal and personal, transcendent and immanent. The personal character of reality is evident as we view it in relation to the world and the individual self. But there is no suggestion of a transcendence of the category of personality in the real in its ultimate state. The real is in its essence also personal. The attribute-possessing (Saguna) God and the attribute-negating (Nirguna) absolute are the same reality. Passages can be extensively quoted from the Upanishads to show how in the upanishadic view there is no negation of the personality of the ultimate. There is no need for the transcendence of personality, for the personality which the ultimate is, is free from the limitations of human personality. Rather the acknowledgement of the ultimate as the perfected personality is necessary, because it makes the manifestation of the ultimate in the world and the individual self possible. The Upanishads consistently maintain that the world is the expression or the manifestation of the absolute or God, which means that the world is itself real; for the manifestation of the real cannot be unreal. The concept 'Māyā' occurs in the upanishadic literature. But Māyāvāda, i.e. the doctrine of the unreality of the world, is alien to the Upanishads. In the upanishadic view, the absolute is admitted as the creator and preserver of the world. Now the world's creator and preserver is all-powerful and all-knowing. That the absolute is the creator or the lord of the world, and has such metaphysical attributes as omnipotence and omniscience, means that there is no essential distinction between the absolute (Brahman) and God (Īśvara). It is only when emphasizing the transcendence of the absolute that reference is made to the abstractness and impersonality of the ultimate. There is no risk in this emphasis, for it is intended as a corrective to the one-sided (pantheistic) identification of God with the world. Thus in the Upanishads we have the characterization of the absolute as personal with the essential metaphysical attributes referred to, and it is a mistake to deny the theistic character of the upanishadic view of the ultimate.

It is interesting to note the affinity between theism as it is found in the Upanishads and in Christianity. The upanishadic characterization of God as the creator and the lord of the world, and as omnipotent and omniscient, is similar to the Christian view of God. The two conceptions of God – the upanishadic and the Christian – differ in one essential respect in that the former stresses the metaphysical while the latter emphasizes the moral qualities of God. The theism of the Upanishads is more developed in the later Hindu scriptures, i.e. the Bhagavad-Gītā, so far as the latter focuses on the moral attributes of God and recognizes devotion (Bhakti) as the principal mode of union with Him. We have a completely developed

theism in the later Hindu schools of theistic Vedānta and Vaiṣṇavism which, like Christian theism, lay emphasis on the moral attributes of God, such as goodness, benevolence, and love. There are
some historians of Indian philosophy who even speak of the influence of Christianity upon the schools referred to.

It is pointed out that the interpreters who characterize the Hindu
view of the ultimate reality as abstract refer to Vedānta (Śaṅkara
Vedānta) in defence of their interpretation. I may make two
observations by way of criticism of this reference to Śaṅkara-
Vedānta : (a) to select one of the different schools of Vedānta and
to view it as representative of the whole of vedāntic thought is
unjustified; and (b) Śaṅkara-Vedānta does not claim to be a religious
view at all, for religion itself is relegated to the level of appearance,
which is transcended or negated from the standpoint of the ultimate.
To take up each of these observations. There are schools of Vedānta
that are opposed to the pure monism of Śaṅkara-Vedānta. It is
therefore, wrong to treat the latter as if it were *the* Vedānta. Theistic
Vedānta and Vaiṣṇava theism are more representative of the
practising faith of the Hindus than is Śaṅkara-Vedānta. Indeed
contemporary Hinduism is characterized by an opposition to
Śaṅkara-Vedānta. Sri Aurobindo's rejection of Māyāvāda, i.e. the
doctrine of the unreality of the world, is a case in point. To come
to the second observation, the Advaita view of ultimate reality,
associated with Śaṅkara, is not a religious view at all, for it considers religion as a matter of ignorance (Avidyā). This is evident
from the view of the strong central distinction between the absolute
of philosophy (Brahman) and the God (Īśvara) of religion. The
absolute is an abstract and attributeless identity, while God is a
determinate identity – one possessing qualities. It is the personal
God who is the object of prayer and worship. It is, therefore, wrong
to characterize Śaṅkara-Vedānta as pantheistic, because pantheism
views God as impersonal and as the ultimate. God, in Sankara's
view, is neither impersonal nor ultimate. Thus A. S. Geden, in the
Encyclopaedia of Religion and Ethics, wrongly maintains that 'So
far from denying that there is a God, the Vedānta identifies everything with Him' (vol. 6, p. 285). (By Vedānta, Geden means Śaṅkara-
Vedānta.) I say 'wrongly' since Śaṅkara maintains that God is not
real from the ultimate standpoint.

The interpreters who misrepresent the Hindu view of the ultimate
also commit an error of omission in that they ignore the scriptures
and the systems in which the theistic conception of God or the

ultimate is extensively developed. We can say that the Gītā is to the Hindus what the Bible is to the Christians and the Qur'ān is to the Muslims. The Gītā is the most popular Hindu scripture and it is unfortunate that many Western interpreters of Hinduism do not take much notice of it. In the Gītā the theistic character of the Upanishads is fully developed. God is characterized as paramātman (the Supreme Self). The Supreme Self is viewed as the lord of the world. The theism of the Gītā represents an advance on that of the Upanishads is fully developed. God is characterized as paramātman God is viewed as the supremely moral being. He is characterized as just, benevolent, and kind. To quote a verse, 'Even as a mother is not unkind to her children whether she fondles or beats them, so also Īśvara – God – the determiner of good and evil is not unkind'. God is also characterized as love. In the Bhaktimārga (the pre-scribed path of devotion), which is so basic to the Gītā, reference is often made to the need for the loving approach to the loving God. 'That he who loveth me shall not perish'. We have a still further development of Hindu theism in the theistic Vedānta (the school of Rāmānuja) in that in this school we have the greater stress on the moral qualities of God. Rāmānuja, the founder of the theistic Vedānta, which flourished in South India about A.D. 1000, claims that in upholding theism he is following the Upanishads and the other scriptures. Rāmānuja characterizes God as the Paramapurusha (the Supreme Person) having different attributes. He emphasizes the moral qualities of God. One principal moral quality is love. God is in essence love (*Karuṇā*). It is an act of loving that is the motive for the creation of the world. Love is not a mere emotion but is the supreme value – goodness. This is directed to the fulfilment of the moral need of man, and that is why God is characterized as the friend, the one on whom man can depend. God is intimately related to man. Rāmānuja, of course, refers to the metaphysical attributes of God, such as omniscience and omnipotence. But the stress is laid on his moral qualities – justice, kindness, and love. In the emphasis on the loving and intimate relation between God and man the distinctiveness of the former is not lost sight of. That is, God is regarded as both immanent and transcendent. The divine-human love is mutual. Man can be in union with God in an attitude of devotion (Bhakti). This devotion or love is possible in an attitude of total surrender (*prapatti*) to God. In Vaiṣṇavism, which is anticipated in the theistic Vedānta of Rāmānuja, the devotional and loving approach to the God of love is completely developed.

The Vaiṣṇavic love is different from the love of which Rāmānuja speaks, to the extent that it is more in the nature of an emotion. This is evident from the reference to sweet love (Mādhurya), or love of God as one's lover, as the highest love. Five types of love are recognized: Śānta (peaceful love), Dāsya (servant of God), Sākhya (friendship with God), Vātsalya (filial love), and Mādhurya. In both Rāmānuja's system and Vaiṣṇavism there is reference to heaven as the eternal abode of God. Thus in the evolution of the development of Hindu theism that can be traced in the Vedas and the Upanishads, we notice a transition from stress on the metaphysical attributes of God to a stress on love as the essence of God via emphasis on His moral attributes.

It appears from this brief survey of the Hindu conception of God or the ultimate reality that it is theistic, and that it is wrong to characterize it as abstract and negative. Hinduism and Christianity as theistic religions are naturally similar in certain respects. It is evident that the similarity between Hindu theism, as we find it in Rāmānuja's school and in Vaiṣṇavism, and Christian theism, is more striking in view of the agreement in their stress on the moral attributes of God, such as love. One important point of difference between the two, however, is that the latter, unlike the former, focuses on the forgiving and the redeeming character of the divine love. The emphasis on the connection between forgiveness and love has its source in the Christian assumption of the sinful character of the natural existence of man. But recognition of the common ground between Hinduism and Christianity renders obsolete the language of contrast between the Hindu and the Christian views of ultimate reality.

It is equally misleading to contrast the Hindu view of the world with the Christian, or for that matter, the western view of the world. Many western interpreters characterize the former as world-negating. A deeper study of Hinduism reveals that this attempted contrast between the two views of the world is not tenable.

The Hindu View of the World

The interpreters who characterize the Hindu view of the world in negatives refer in defence of their position to (a) the Māyāvāda or the doctrine of the unreality of the world, and (b) the practical Hindu attitude of indifference to the world. I will examine each of these considerations. Māyāvāda, or the doctrine of the unreality of the world, is the thesis of one of the many systems of Hindu thought, i.e. of the pure monism of Śaṅkara's school; and it is erroneous, as we have already observed, to interpret the whole of Hinduism in the light of one system or school. An objective understanding of Hinduism is possible if we study closely the different Hindu systems and find the beliefs that are dominant in them. It is patent that the dominant Hindu belief is not a belief in the unreality of the world. Māyāvāda is alien to the scriptures – the Vedas, the Upanishads, and the Gītā. The concept 'Māyā', occurs only rarely in the 'classical' Upanishads. But Māyāvāda is not upheld in any one of the Upanishads. There are, of course, certain negative passages in the upanishadic literature that indicate the notion of all-exclusive reality (*niṣprapañca Brahman*). These passages, it may be pointed out, need to be understood in the light of an emphasis on the transcendent character of God – the supreme reality. In the Gītā there is no reference to the unreality or the illusory character of the world. Five of the six systems of Hindu philosophy are world-affirming. The sixth system, i.e. the Vedānta, as has been observed, admits of different types and only one of these is world-negating. The other types are characterized by the rejection of Māyāvāda. It is no exaggeration to state that it is not the affirmation but the negation of Māyāvāda that is more characteristic of Hinduism. Sri Aurobindo, the most noted recent Hindu philosopher, in his *The Life Divine*, bases his interpretation of Hinduism on the extensive and effective refutation of Mayavada. In the scripture and in the different systems of Hinduism, except of course the pure monistic system, the world is characterized as an expression or manifestation of the supreme reality, and it is evident that an expression or a manifestation of the real cannot be unreal.

Some critics of the Hindu view of the world say that even if Hinduism is free from Māyāvāda, Hindu religious believers have a keen sense of the insubstantiality and the limitations of the world. This observation, however, is not tenable, for the sense of the insubstantiality of the world, which is another name for the sense of the contingency of the world, is not peculiar to Hindu religious believers, but is something that religious believers of all traditions have in common. Awareness of the limitations and the dependence of the world marks the beginning of religious consciousness. Indeed religious consciousness originates in the sense of dissatisfaction with the limitations of the world. To one who is satisfied with the world, believing that it is independent and ultimate, religion is impossible. There is, therefore, no point in saying that it is the Hindus who alone express the sense of the insubstantiality and dependence of the world. It is also pointed out that Hindu religious believers, vis-à-vis western religious believers, are committed to the ideal of non-attachment, which is essentially the ideal of withdrawal from the world. It may be said in reply that non-attachment to the world does not mean an escape or a flight from it. It means participation in the world and life's activities in a disinterested way. The attitude of non-attachment is characterized by an attitude of being in the world but not of it.

We come now to the second attempted contrast between the Hindu view of the world and the Christian view. It is said that Hindus uphold the message of non-action, and exhibit a practical attitude of indifference to the world. The belief underlying this indifference to the world is said to be pessimism. It is supposed that the world is so full of sorrow that human action, however radical or revolutionary, cannot make any difference to what the world inherently is. If, therefore, I am to hope at all, I need to look beyond this world. My observations in reply to this challenge are as follows: (a) Hindus do not uphold the ethics of non-action. This is evident from the place of the Gītā's *Karma Yoga* (devotion to action) in Hindu religious thought. What is recommended is not the renunciation of action but of the fruits or the results of the action. (b) There is no truth in the characterization of Hinduism as pessimistic. The belief that admits the suffering of the world but prescribes a way of redemption from it is not pessimism. Pessimism regards human suffering as ultimate, and cannot have a message of liberation. Hinduism, on the other hand, throughout upholds liberation (Mokṣa) as the ultimate goal, and consistently maintains that it is emancipation in the world and not from it.

The Hindu View of Liberation

It is asserted that in the Hindu view, liberation is a spiritual state of the realization of ultimate reality, and is transcendent in character. Further, the ethical sphere pertains to the phenomenal and lower level and is transcended as one attains liberation. The experience has no ethical content in that it is an awareness of what transcends value. That is, one who is liberated is free from commitment to moral actions such as self-sacrifice and benevolence for others. It is contended that the spiritual experience is independent of moral experience not only because of its transcendent character but also in respect of its essentially cognitive character. Liberation as the discovery of the nature of the real is in the nature of a cognition, and has nothing to do with moral action. The spiritual experience is also independent and autonomous in that it is not ethically conditioned. That is, Karma (moral action) is not a necessary condition for the attainment of liberation. One need not indulge in actions of a certain type, such as serving and loving others, for one's emancipation. It is said that, in the Christian view, liberation is love, whereas in the Hindu view, one cannot say that to be liberated is to love. It is also stated in this connection that the Hindu ethic is negative in character in that it upholds the ideal of self-denial as an end in itself.

Now the view that Hindu religion affirms the non-ethical character of spiritual experience on the basis of its transcendent and cognitive character is not tenable, for it treats of only *one* Hindu view of liberation (the view associated with the pure monism of the Advaita school) as *the* Hindu view. The Advaita view characterizes liberation as a transcendent state in which what is ethical is transcended or negated. The characterization of liberation in negatives follows from the Advaita ontology, which regards the ultimate reality as transcendent and all-exclusive. Now Hindu religious believers, as we have already observed, reject the Advaita ontology to the extent that they affirm the infinite as divine person, having moral attributes such as goodness, justice, love, etc. And the state of realization of the supreme person who is unlimited in goodness and love has, by the nature of the case, an ethical content. A contrast between the liberating spiritual awareness and moral awareness has, therefore, no place. The spiritual awareness has an elevating and transforming effect on life. One who is liberated can claim moral excellence insofar as he fulfils the supreme value which the ultimate or God is, more adequately than one who is bound. The way of liberation does not mark the cessation of the way of action, for liberation in the world is possible. For liberated persons, living in the world means performing actions, for to live is to act. All that we can say is that with liberation there is a change of activity, to the extent that the moral life is the life of conflict and resistance for one who is in bondage, while it is natural and spontaneous for one who is emancipated. It is significant that the liberated souls belonging to different Hindu organizations exert a supremely moral influence on ordinary believers. It is contended that liberation is knowledge insofar as it involves a disclosure of the nature of the relation between one's self and God, the ultimate reality. The knowledge in which liberation consists is essentially different from ordinary knowledge, because it is devotion to what is considered as the object of ultimate concern, so that in it knowledge and value interpenetrate. It is maintained that knowledge partakes of the nature of being. To know God is to be God. But the state of being one with God is not one of complete absorption into the divine or the ultimate reality. In the Hindu view, liberation, which has an ethical content, is also ethically conditioned. Liberation is a matter of attainment through moral actions. The strict Hindu position is that liberation does not come as a gift. We know that in the Christian view, liberation is a matter of grace. To whom and when grace comes depends on the divine will itself. The Christian doctrine of grace renders the religious and the ethical spheres discontinuous and disconnected. We do not know how a religion that claims to be essentially ethical can view liberation as a matter af grace. Hindu religious believers maintain that one principal way of attaining emancipation is moral action – the other ways being Jñānayoga (the path of knowledge) and Bhaktiyoga (the path of devotion). The difference between one system and another is in their varying emphases. It is, therefore, wrong to say that in the Hindu view the path of Karma is ignored. The Gītā emphasizes strongly the path of action.

One criticism of Hindu religious belief (to which reference has been made) is that moral action, which is admitted as a necessary means to the attainment of liberation, is negative in that it is of the nature of self-denial. That is, the positive moral life as constituted of altruistic acts, such as justice, benevolence, and love, is ignored. In the words of A. C. Bouquet 'The world renouncing ascetic is the type universally admired, and his renunciation is in no sense altruistic or philanthropic'. This criticism is not valid, for the Hindu view of dharma (moral life), which can claim to be elaborate and comprehensive, acknowledges the importance of altruistic actions. This is particularly evident from the detailed list of duties that are prescribed. Besides, we know of many religious leaders, the foremost among whom is Swami Vivekananda, who have through their extensive social reforms tried to show that the ideal of social service is not alien to Hindu religion. Gandhiji was basically a Hindu spiritualist who dedicated himself completely to the cause of social justice. Bouquet remarks that 'Gandhiji was notably inconsistent when he made unselfish service to his fellow men a part of the discipline to which he subjected himself in order to free his soul from the bonds of flesh since self-forgetful service to others is a Christian not a Hindu idea'. The remark is typical of the attempted contrast between Hinduism and Christianity against which this paper is directed. The point of this brief survey of the Hindu view of liberation is that liberation cannot be characterized in negatives, as contrasted with the Christian view. The moral of this inquiry into the nature of the misrepresentation of Hinduism is that it is misleading to contrast one religion with another in an aggressive or exclusive spirit.

Finally, I shall try to indicate briefly the nature and the extent of the agreement or connectedness between different religions. To do so is not, however, to assimilate one religion to another; for the agreement between religions is an agreement between distinct entities.

The agreement or the connectedness between different religions is not contingent. This is, we cannot say that it so happens that religious believers belonging to different faiths agree in certain essential ways. The agreement is necessary insofar as is arises from what I call the religious situation, i.e. that in which religious believers qua believers are involved, and from the natural connection between this situation and the structure of human existence. The ontological explanation of the agreement, i.e. an explanation on the assumption that the different religions are responses to one divine reality, is not tenable, since it is question-begging. It is necessary to establish that the reality is divine and that there is one divine reality. It is only on the basis of the belief in a common religious situation that we can legitimately talk of a common religious discourse and of the possibility of a philosophy of religion that presupposes a common religious discourse. We have already observed that to study a religion as an abstraction is to misapprehend the nature of a religion and to miss its connection with other religions. Each religion is to be viewed as a human phenomenon relative to a particular situational complex in the cultural life of a people. Now to study one situational complex in isolation from another is to commit the error of abstraction. What is necessary is that one situational complex should be apprehended in relation to another within a common religious situation in which all are naturally involved. This common religious situation, connected with the nature and structure of the finite existence of man, has different components: (a) the fact of finitude, (b) the consciousness or awareness of finitude, (c) the urge for the transcendence of inherently limited existence, (d) the transcendence to what is unlimited and infinite. It is on the basis of this insight into the situation that we can explain the essential points of agreement or connectedness between different religions, which are (a) God- or infinite-centredness, (b) ontological commitment, and (c) ethical commitment. To develop each of these points: (a) the different religions are God- or Infinite-centred. The distinctive character of the accepted usage of the concept 'religion' is in the recognition of the centrality of the infinite, i.e. that which transcends or overcomes the limitedness which is inherent in the nature and structure of human existence. This indicates that religious consciousness originates in the awareness of and dissatisfaction with the limitedness of finitude, which is inherent in human existence itself. Man is conscious that he is limited and that his state of limitedness cannot be overcome on the human plane. Now this consciousness that is the prerogative of man naturally involves a sense of dissatisfaction and the need to overcome it through a yearning for the unlimited and the infinite, and this yearning is another name for transcendence. It follows, therefore, that the object of religious consciousness is the infinite or God. It is believed that transcendence to the infinite or God lends fullness of meaning to man's existence and to his life's activities, and that is why God or the infinite is recognized, not merely as the ground of the world but also as the goal of human actions. Religious believers, however, disagree on the nature of the infinite. This is not the place to go into the nature of the disagreement. It is, however, relevant to point out that a recognition of the unlimited and the infinite is common to different religions.

(b) The different religions evince a common ontological commitment, i.e. a commitment to the belief in the reality or the beingness of the infinite or God. That God is real or, to put it negatively, is not non-being, is a thesis on which the varying faiths agree. This agreement is not a contingent fact but is necessary to the nature of religious belief, and to the mode of religious conduct consisting of worship and prayer. I have tried to show this in my book, *Transcendence, Mystery and Maya* (Calcutta, 1968). I can only indicate here that the belief in God as the ground of the world and the goal of human aspirations, unless it is make-believe – which, however, it is not – cannot be belief in the non-existent. The ontological commitment may be explicit or implicit. It is made explicit in the wake of denials of the reality of the object of belief, and of the reactions of the religious believers to this. The attempts of some modern empiricists (R. B. Braithwaite and others) to affirm religion in dissociation from this ontological claim, amounts to a violation of the nature of religious believing.

(c) Each of the different religions involves an ethical commitment. There is no religious scripture that does not indicate the nature of good conduct and does not have an extensive list of duties or prescriptions. The language of prayer and worship is also the language of an appeal to God – the benevolent power whose guidance and assistance in the realization of ideals makes good living possible. That each religion has an ethical commitment is not contingent, for it is intelligible and explicable only on the presupposition of the religious situation I have referred to. The infinite or the ultimate, as we have already observed, is not merely the ground of the world, but is also the supreme goal of ethical efforts. It is in a union with the infinite that is also the ultimate that human liberation consists. That each religion has a corresponding view of liberation is significant and indicative of its essential ethical commitment, though the nature of this commitment is not the same in all religions. For instance, in one religion, emphasis is on the ethics of self-control while, in another religion, the stress is on the ethics of love.

I have so far tried to indicate briefly the areas of agreement among different religions. We have already observed that this agreement is between distinct entities. Each religion has its distinctive character in respect both of belief and of conduct. A proper understanding of religions is possible if their distinctive characters are studied in the light of these areas of agreement. Such a study reveals that their distinctive characteristics are in the nature of differences in emphasis. The different religions should be approached in the belief that their distinctive emphases are complementary to one another. The adherent of one religious faith can draw on what another faith offers to him. There is no doubt that the different religions are only enriched in the process of mutual adaptation. For instance, a Hindu is no less a Hindu in his openness or adaptation to what he finds in Christianity and misses in his own religion. On the contrary, his faith is enriched and he stands on stronger ground. That no one religion, as also no one thought-pattern, can be a repository of all truths is obvious. What is all the more unfortunate is that experts in different theological circles need to be continually reminded of this truth. In an attitude of openness to other religions, and a readiness to draw on them, there can be a fruitful dialogue. We must create the conditions to ensure conversation between persons having diverse beliefs and faiths in a spirit of trust, sympathy, and appreciation. Such a climate of increasing conversation or dialogue will, in addition to its bearing on the attainment of truth, contribute to the fulfilment of the ideal of human unity. For perhaps the greatest human predicament is that religion, with its essential commitment to universality, has been a divisive force. It is the supreme irony that the supposed children of God have fallen apart in the name of God. Our hope is that we are today more aware of the gap between what religion is and what it can be, and that we have set ourselves to overcome the gap.

SANTOSH SENGUPTA is Professor of Philosophy and Head of the Centre of Advanced Study in Philosophy at Visva-Bharati University, India. Author of *An Enquiry into the Existence of God*; *Good, Freewill and God*; *Transcendence, Mystery and Māyā*; *Belief, Faith and Knowledge*, etc.

Is the Bhagavad-Gītā the Word of God?

GEOFFREY PARRINDER

In *Questions of Religious Truth* (1967), lectures given at Yale
Divinity School, Wilfred Cantwell Smith devoted a chapter to the
pointed question, 'Is the Qur'ān the Word of God?' This would be
answered, he said, with an emphatic affirmative as an article of
faith by Muslims, but it would have been almost as strongly denied
by Christians in the past, and today is either repudiated or, worse,
ignored. From a different point of view W. Montgomery Watt, in
Islamic Revelation in the Modern World (1969), p. 8, confesses, as
an 'amateur' Christian theologian, that 'I hold the Qur'ān to be in
some sense the product of a divine initiative and therefore revelation'.

Islam is much closer to Christianity than is Hinduism, and it is
easier to consider the Qur'ān from the standpoint of western
philosophy or Christian theology, than it is to undertake a similar
consideration of an Indian scripture. My chief excuse must be that
for the past twelve years I have held an annual series of seminars
for the study of the Bhagavad-Gītā, prescribed in the London degree
syllabus, and feel that this inspiring but complex scripture raises
acute problems for us. There are, of course, plenty of other Hindu
texts, but the Gītā is central and easily accessible, and we can now
use R. C. Zaehner's massive commentary and translation, *The
Bhagavad-Gītā* (1969), perhaps the most important critical and
theological commentary made in modern times on any non-Biblical
text.

It may be objected, at least by students of the comparative study
of religions, that such a theological discussion is unnecessary. Do
we not all assume that these books, Qur'ān and Gītā, are divinely
inspired because we read and teach them? To this, one answer is
that all too often, as will be said later, such books are taken as
texts for study or analysis but their religious value is easily ignored,
either for Hindus in the past or for us today. It is also true that some
Christians, especially in the Indian churches, use the Gītā and
other selected Indian scriptures, and are prepared to regard them

as divine revelations, yet such an attitude is still foreign, or not explicit, to theologians in general. Therefore, some of the leading teachings and attitudes of the Gītā will now be selected for consideration, in order to see if they can be embraced within the concept of revelation from a theological rather than a philosophical viewpoint.

Divine Speech

The Bhagavad-Gītā claims to be the 'Lord's Song' by Krishna, the Bhagavat, who appears in its seven hundred verses as supreme God. It purports to be revelation, where prose introductions state that 'the blessed Lord said' (*Śrībhagavān uvāca*). In the ensuing verses, Krishna replies to Arjuna's problems on fighting and action in general. That the Blessed Lord speaks at all, is remarkable and unusual at this point in the development of the Hindu scriptures (somewhere between the fifth and second centuries B.C.). In the older and formally more revered Vedas, there are many hymns to the gods. They are Songs of Praise, or Psalms in some ways comparable to what the Hebrew Psalters may have been before they were expurgated in the interests of monotheism. Priests chant the praises of the deities, imploring them to hear and come down to enjoy the sacrifices. It is to be presumed that the gods were thought to answer and descend, but their words are not recorded, apart from a few verses where some abstract character, such as Vāc, the word, speaks about itself. God does not speak to man in the Vedas, the action is all the other way, godward and not manward. No doubt the Psalter is rather similar, also godward, and to hear the challenge of 'thus saith the Lord', we have to wait for the prophets. But prophetic influence appears in the Psalms and there is a closeness of divine-human relationships that is rarely seen in the Vedas.

In the Indian priestly and speculative books, Brāhmaṇas and Upanishads, there is even less clear claim to revelation. Preoccupation with the minutiae of sacrifice seems to lead to magical rather than mystical religion, and there are few more tedious works than these priestly handbooks, which put even Leviticus in the shade. Then the groping speculations of the Upanishads have profound moments, but a growing tendency towards monistic pantheism does not provide a congenial setting for divine revelation. The classic and repeated declaration, 'thou art That', excludes divine-human dialogue. It is true that later Hinduism called these Vedas and Brāhmaṇas, and even the Upanishads, *śruti*, 'heard' by the sages from the gods, but formally and critically they do not read like revelation.

Against this background, and that of agnostic Buddhism and Sāṁkhya, appeared the Bhagavad-Gītā, emerging strangely from the riotous mythology of the epic Mahābhārata. Here the claim is openly made that God speaks to man, and if it is the first time it has also been called the last in Hinduism. There are many other texts where deities address men, but generally in a more derivative and less sustained manner. Krishna rarely teaches in the other didactic verses of the Mahābhārata. In the fourteenth book is the Anugītā, the repeated or 'after-song', in which much of the less distinctive teaching of the Bhagavad-Gītā is recapitulated. But while Krishna (Vāsudeva) speaks again, here much of the Anugītā is by other characters, chiefly Brahmins, and a growing monism reduces the impact of divine revelation. In Śaivite schools there is, for example, the Īśvara-Gītā (Lord's Song) from the Kūrma Purāna, which is clearly based upon the Bhagavad-Gītā. Here once again the Lord spoke (*Īśvara uvāca*) but at shorter length, eleven chapters compared with eighteen, and much of it repeating the older work. It is significant that the more pantheistic chapters nine and ten are partly copied from the Bhagavad-Gītā, but the Avatar and the transcendental version are not mentioned in the Īśvara-Gītā.

Word and Event

The Bhagavad-Gītā stands out then like a great peak above the plains of monism and the foothills of polytheistic mythology. Here God speaks to man and while there is complexity, and some mystification, yet there is no doubt of the claim to present revealed truth.

But who is this God and what does he say? The divinities (*devas*) of Hinduism were innumerable, yet there had long appeared an urge to reduce their diversity to unity, the tendency towards a form of monotheism which might be paralleled in different ways in ancient Israel and Greece. Whatever were the origins of Krishna, perhaps a 'black' god of Dravidian tribes, and whatever the attraction of his later erotic adventures with the milkmaids, in the Gītā he is the lofty deity teaching morality. It is recognized that men worship other gods, and Krishna is a god who is sometimes called *deva*, though he is also Primal God, *ādi-deva* (11.38). Moreover not only is worship of other gods inferior, 'deprived of wisdom by many desires men turn to other gods', and this will bring rebirth, yet the faith of such devotees is really inspired by Krishna himself and so their worship is to God alone (7.20f.; 9.23).

God speaks to man in the Gītā, and Krishna is primarily the Guru, the teacher of Yoga and Lord of Yoga. His revelations are partly in a series of propositions, for example, asserting the indestructibility of the soul or the duties of the social classes. But these are not mere theories, they always have a practical bearing, encouraging Arjuna to do his duty and maintain order for the welfare of the world. One dominant meaning of Yoga, among many shifts of emphasis, is so to integrate oneself as to perform duty without attachment to rewards or fear of punishment.

Yet revelation in the Gītā is not simply the enunciation of propositions, it is the declaration of divine as well as human action. Some of the most famous verses announce the divine Avatar, the appearance of God in visible form in the world (4.6-9). The theory of Avatars, 'descents' or incarnations of the deity, had been announced earlier in the Mahābhārata, and the word *avatāra* itself does not occur in the Gītā though the belief is there. One reason given for men to be active is because of God's own activity (3.22f.), yet God is not forced to action by any Karma. Similarly, although he is unborn and the lord of beings, yet to maintain the balance of right (*dharma*), the lord comes to birth by his own power 'age after age'.

This Avatar doctrine has often been compared with the Christian doctrine of the incarnation, though there are clear differences (see my *Avatar and Incarnation*). The Avatar is a theophany, an appearance of God to men, and herein lies its value as teaching the divine activity in this world to restore righteousness. The Gītā says very little else about it, and even in other Hindu legends of Krishna and Rāma these visible gods are hardly limited men who really suffer and die. Nevertheless, of all the teachings in the world's religions, the Avatar doctrines are closest to those of the incarnation. They are revelation as event, a visible as well as a spoken word of God.

In later times it was said that there appeared a different Avatar of the supreme Vishnu in every age. The Gītā does not indicate that, and it is the same blessed lord who appears throughout the ages, thus reaffirming the fundamental monotheism of the book. This monotheism is powerfully reinforced by the transcendental vision which appears in chapter eleven and is perhaps the most tremendous and fascinating vision to be found in all religious literature. In the vision the name God, with a capital G, must be justified. Krishna is the lord of gods, the first creator and ancient spirit (Purusha), above the neuter Brahman, the all, the origin and dissolution of the whole cosmic process.

There are few Hindu expressions of faith (later Śaiva Siddhānta perhaps excepted) which have a clearer monotheism. And if to those of us from the Semitic traditions there may seem to be many lesser spirits still in evidence in the Gītā, it may be suggested that a too transcendental monotheism also tends to produce its own angels, saints and shaikhs, to fill the yawning gap between God and man. At least the Gītā has something of the dogmatism that is often associated with monotheism. It has been called an 'uncompromising eirenicon' (Hill), trying to appease the orthodox and the popular schools, the Vedas (though with some biting criticisms) and the Upanishads, Sāṃkhya, and Yoga. But this is done, sometimes subtly and sometimes bluntly, by declaring Krishna to be the God of gods, the author of Veda and Vedānta, the owner of Sāṃkhya Prakriti (nature) and the highest spirit (Purushottama), the lord of Yoga which he taught from the beginning, the only giver of grace and the true object of devotion. He founded the order of caste, upholds morality, and is the only saviour from transmigration; for whereas worshippers of other gods will return to earth again, the lovers of Krishna will be fully delivered from the dying round. So it clearly appears that the claims made for Krishna as the only God are as absolute as those for Yahweh or Allah.

Grace and Love

It is not possible in a short paper to examine the many and intricate subjects that appear in the Gītā, on which countless commentaries have been written though, as R. C. Zaehner points out, many of them in the past and at present were written from a monistic standpoint, which is about the worst position for understanding the theology of the Gītā. It must suffice to indicate a few teachings that seem important for considering the Gītā as a divine revelation.

First of all, its theology, which is often under-estimated in looking for philosophy or Yoga. Krishna, it has been said, is presented as the supreme and really the sole deity. In the India of that time such a teaching was a great achievement. The Buddha has often been called an atheist, or a transtheist or transpolytheist, but the weakness of the first two at least is that apparently there was no supreme 'theos' for him to accept or reject in the Hinduism of the fifth century B.C. The Gītā, in the manner that has been sketched above, now begins to unite many teachings and concepts to produce a faith in one God. It does more, it gives a convincing picture of a God who is at once almighty and merciful. It is striking, and surely significant to us in the Semitic traditions, that when Arjuna hails Krishna as the supreme, the all, and offers sixfold homage (11.39f.), he follows this immediately by a confession of his own unworthiness. This is sin against God, and not the usual evil or trouble of the Indian scriptures. Arjuna has been over-familiar with the visible Krishna, negligent or disrespectful, in play, rest, eating, and sitting, publicly and privately, and so he begs forgiveness. He prostrates himself and asks for mercy from God as father, friend and lover. Indeed the vision of God, with all the attributes of the celestial Vishnu, proves too much and having asked for the sight he now pleads for a return to the normal divine-human form. The author of the book of Job had a similar thought about the same time (Job 42.5). This self-abasement before the transcendental vision is followed by divine grace, and God comforts his frightened follower by showing again his gracious aspect.

It is hardly surprising that this majesty, terror, and grace are followed in the next chapter by open declarations of the love of God. The Vedas assumed that the gods would make some response to human appeals and they were asked to be kindly disposed; sometimes they are called father and friend, but there is no deeper love. Even less could the Brahman 'without qualities' of the Upanishads demonstrate any concern even for the ascetic sage with whom it was identical. Only when theism enters again does affection increase. It is the Gītā that pleads with God to show mercy, 'as a lover to his beloved' (11.44). There is a growing stress on *bhakti* (devotion-love) from the worshipper to God, and signs that the feeling is reciprocated. This is hinted at quite early, 'I return their love' (*bhajāmy aham*, 4.11), but it is in the chapter of Bhakti that the divine response is most emphasized. In five success-ive verses the devotee is called 'dear' to God, or 'loved in return' (*sa me priyaḥ*, 12.14-20), and finally 'dear beyond measure' or 'loved exceedingly'. And in the climax of the last chapter the highest and supreme word is that the worshipper is 'greatly loved' by God (*ishto'si*, 18.64).

The Gītā has sometimes been compared with the New Testament, and the slow way in which it arrived at love was reckoned to its disadvantage. But a more apposite comparison would be with the

Old Testament, where against a similarly unpromising background the belief in the love of God slowly emerged in the prophets, notably in Hosea, though there it is communal rather than individual. The Gītā, of course, has none of the eroticism that in the Purāṇas the medieval Indian poetry both enriched and at times degraded the concept of divine love for human beings. But it provides the starting point for belief in a God who cares and is able to save, beyond the stream of transmigration and over the power of Karma.

Soul or Self

One can hardly ignore the basic belief of the Gītā in the indestructibility of the soul. This is the first answer to Arjuna's problems and it is in line with traditional Upanishadic and Sāṁkhya teaching (2.20). Belief in the eternity of the soul, pre-existent as well as post-existent, is fundamental to Hindu thought and is different from, and perhaps opposed to, Christian belief in immortality. It seems to be, or at least it can be (in Sāṁkhya), independent of belief in God. The everlasting souls are unborn, proceed from one embodiment to another, and finally by detachment attain to Brahman-Nirvāṇa, a term apparently invented by the Gītā (2.72).

Yet as the theism of the Gītā develops so does the strong link of God with human souls. It is not surprising that Otto, in his *Original Gītā* (E.T. 1939), singled out the transcendental vision of chapter eleven as one of the few basic elements of the book, but passed direct to here from chapter two. The theology of the vision brings a radical change of emphasis, where God is not just the soul in all beings but the primal creator (11.37; 10.20). All beings are passing into him in the pyre of dissolution and no doubt will emerge from him in the next cycle. It is after this chapter that there appears the new idea that men are not saved simply by works or knowledge, by the Vedas or asceticism, but by a God of grace: 'I will lift them up', or be their 'saviour' from the round of deaths (12.7).

The doctrine of transmigration, so foreign to the Semitic traditions, is fundamental to the Indian. And if one were to criticize the Gītā as word of God, from the Semitic viewpoint, one would rather begin here than with the variant theistic emphases. And yet the notion of Karma which, rightly or wrongly, provides a facile explanation of the ills of life, is not such an endless burden if it is seriously modified by the popularity of the religions of love, faith, and grace. The Avatar cults of Vaishṇavism, Śaiva Siddhānta, and Pure Land Buddhism may have been regarded as superstitious or 'short cut' religions by the ascetic and philosophical, but they have had something of the true stuff of religion in them. The apparent world-denial of Indian philosophy contrasts strangely with the great Indian cultures and works of art, and the inspiration for much of the latter may be credited to the devotional religions.

Morality

Ethics appears to be essential to religion, for those cradled in Semitic monotheism. The Gītā too has a great concern with duty, since this is its very first word (*dharmakshetre*), though at the end its fervour of devotion tells Arjuna to 'abandon all dharmas' (18.66). It is a book of Dharma, and one of its greatest contributions to Indian thought is the insistence that men must work; not even an ascetic can cease all activity, and God himself is in constant action (3.5, 22). There is as much scorn expressed for penances as for Vedic rituals, and man must act both to perform his class duty and because nature really will not do anything else. Determinism peeps through occasionally, though generally the stress is upon effort.

Yet much of the morality inculcated in the Gītā seems to be cold and detached, the same to foe and friend and above good and evil. This has useful results in regarding a Brahmin as the same as an outcaste (5.18), but it has little of the warmth of love that might have been expected from a book that insists on love to God. Human affection gets little place; Arjuna must kill his foes knowing that their souls are eternal, which is cold comfort for their bodies, and there is no attempt at answering the problem of the compassion of Arjuna, mentioned at the beginning and never raised again. Only occasionally are Yogis said to 'delight in the welfare of all beings' (5.25), a verse popular in the later Mahābhārata but rare in the Gītā.

The ethics of the Gītā appears to be concerned with individual salvation on the one hand, and with the maintenance of class-order on the other, with recommendations to perform one's own duty badly rather than another's duty well for fear of upsetting the balance of society. Nevertheless, as Indians often stress, the Gītā is the supreme teaching of unselfish action, performance of duty in detachment from its fruits, without the bribe of heaven or the threat of hell.

Word of God?

These sketchy reflections on a few doctrines of the Gītā, out of its many stimulating themes, are put forward to help discussion of the status of the Gītā, not merely in Hinduism but for other religions. If one may ask whether the Qur'ān is the word of God, may the same question be asked about the Gītā? Or is it the wrong kind of question, inappropriate, insoluble, irrelevant, or blasphemous? Some effort will now be made to consider the problem, and if it still appears confused afterwards, at least the question will have been raised.

Many Europeans and Americans have read the Gītā, and there are over fifty translations. No doubt the Gītā has been popularly felt to be a good book, instructive and inspiring. But theologians have been reluctant to discuss the issues involved, once the fundamentalist and partly missionary attitudes of dismissing all other religions and their scriptures as sin have been abandoned. On the other hand, academic detachment brings its own problems, in which the sacred texts may in practice find their chief use for exercises in grammar or archaeology. Should not those who teach such scriptures sometimes consider their religious value, not only to their Indian readers but also to themselves? They are not just antiquarian pieces, to be dissected or debunked, and it makes a difference if we can appreciate their religious teachings. Yet the manner in which this is done is too often left undefined and our prejudices remain unexamined.

The Gītā has been claimed to be, and is revered as, the word of God. Men have accepted it as divine, as equivalent to *śruti*, the fifth Veda, and more accessible and comprehensible than the earlier Vedas. When men have read it, in the original or in translations, or have learnt some of its verses by heart, that is because its divine origin was guaranteed.

The Gītā is the word of God to Hindus, and that act of faith determines their approach. But we come to it differently, hearing of its reputation, or accepting it on the recommendation of others, or having it imposed in a university syllabus. We read it first, and make some response, or none, to its divine claims afterwards. We may be attracted by some of its teachings, repelled by others, and perplexed by not a few. Therefore, even if we are prepared to accept part of the Gītā as instructive, inspiring, even divine revelation, it will probably be with many qualifications. Some of the reasons for this must lie with the concept of revelation in our own religion.

That the Gītā, and other scriptures outside the Bible, may contain divine revelation seems to imply that they can mediate salvation to their readers, yet that other religions can be a means of God's salvation is a new, if not heretical, notion. But the important symposium, *Christian Revelation and World Religions* (1967), edited by Joseph Neuner and with chapters by Hans Küng and Raymond Panikkar, contains fresh approaches to the problem. It is not possible to examine these now, but briefly their conviction may be repeated that religions do not save men, not even Christianity does that. Men are saved by God, and the question is whether God uses other religions and scriptures as providential means of salvation. The alternative, that the great masses of mankind have perished in the dark, without any divine revelation, and are all consigned to everlasting hell, is too horrible to contemplate.

Universal Truths

Some of the words of the Gītā may appear inspired to non-Hindus, at least in a general sense. If a statement is true, it must be the word of God. When Arjuna is told that 'action is better than inaction', or that he should 'delight in the welfare of all beings', such exhortations may claim universal assent. Not only were these words true to Rāmānuja, they appear true to us today, so that in an absolute and historic sense some words of the Gītā may be claimed as divine truth.

This is an advance upon the antiquarian study of the book, or a critical dissection of the text in the manner that easily kills the spirit, whether performed upon the Gītā or the New Testament. The Gītā has often been studied for the light that it sheds upon the general culture of India in the third century B.C., or the religious development of Hinduism, without any consideration of its universal truth. In similar fashion European students of the Qur'ān may seek what it can reveal of religion in ancient Arabia, or the ideas of Muhammad, but the Muslim seeks from it the knowledge of God.

Some knowledge of God may perhaps be acknowledged to be obtained from the Gītā, in ethical precepts or general exhortations. But such a recognition of a few general truths may be grudging and superficial. It is still a long way from deep conviction, or from assessing what are the criteria to be applied if the Gītā is to be a word of God to us.

Revelation and Logos

The way in which the Gītā is appraised depends largely upon our own preconceptions, our faith or lack of it. To make an absolute assessment of its value is not possible, for not only would this demand a knowledge of every other scripture with which it might be compared, it would also demand the use of criteria of judgement independent of any particular religion. Enough has been said of the claims of the Gītā to be divine revelation, and the acceptance of these claims by Hindus. It is now time to begin an appraisal from the standpoint of Christian theology.

A Christian theologian ought to be better equipped than an atheist for understanding the Gītā, since he need not dismiss it as mythology or error, and he can seek for some word of God therein. The tragedy has been that in the past, and still to some extent, theologians have rejected or ignored all other scriptures than their own. Yet being a Christian surely implies that God has not left himself without witness, speaking to men 'at sundry times and in divers manners', even outside the Judeo-Christian traditions. If Muslims and Hindus have not had the opportunity of reading the Bible, then the Qur'ān and the Gītā have been the word of God to them. But can they be the word of God to us, and will they endure beside the Bible?

We have been speaking all this time of the Word of God, but what is meant by this term? It is too easy for a Christian to identify the word of God with the Bible, and some modern as well as bygone preachers have introduced scripture reading in church with 'Hear the Word of God'. Yet such an identification of the word with the book is difficult to maintain in the light of modern textual study, and it can also lead to facile comparison and denigration: 'Thy Bible, O Zion, against thy Gītā, O India'.

In the Bible itself it is not any book, but Christ, who is the Word of God, the Logos, the divine utterance, action and incarnation – 'the Word that was in the beginning, the Word that was God, the Word that became flesh.' Bibliolatry, however well-intentioned, detracts from faith in the living Word. Belief in Christ is the distinctive Christian faith, which may be accepted or rejected, but it provides a standard by which a Christian theologian may appreciate claims to have received words from God. Briefly, how far the Gītā may be the word of God for us might be taken to depend, from a Christian viewpoint, upon how far it accords with Christ.

It has been maintained that in the comparison of Christianity and Islam, it is not the Bible but Christ who should be compared with the Qur'ān. The Bible is Hadīth, tradition, and there are four gospels about the one Christ. The comparison is between the Word made flesh and the Word made book. While perhaps this can be taken too far, and too little attention may be paid to the role of Muhammad as an object of devotion, yet the emphasis for Christian theology is important, and not least in discussion of the Gītā.

A Christian theologian who has read and liked the Gītā, and is even prepared to see some divine revelation in it, could justify his sympathy by selecting teachings, such as those singled out above, which appear most congenial to the teachings of Christ: monotheism, grace, love, immortality, and ethics. In justification for such a confessional attitude it may be claimed that men in other religions take up comparable standpoints, as the liberal Muslim may accept Hindus as People of the Book, having sacred scriptures and many of them believing in one God. Yet this can lead to distortion. At a recent international seminar held by the Sikhs at the Punjabi University, Patiala, a Muslim contributor said that Guru Nānak was a monotheist, his conception of God being essentially Islamic, while a Hindu speaker declared that Nānak was not only a pantheist but a monist.

Clearly there are dangers in viewing other people's beliefs through the coloured spectacles of our own religion. Yet it is difficult to know what else the religious believer can do without abandoning his own faith. The indifferentist attitude that could result might, or might not, allow for an understanding of religious philosophy but it would hardly help in the appreciation of devotional religion.

Dialogue

Yet the understanding of another religion or holy book involves listening not only to teachings that confirm beliefs that we already hold, regarding them as confirmation or anticipation of our fuller truth. W. M. Watt has some pointed words on the different kinds of dialogues that are conducted today. Too many of them are conferences at which rival doctrines are expounded, ending with an appeal to the others to consider the superior truth of one's own religion. But for true dialogue a distinction must be made between the positive message of a religion and its defences. The latter always include distortion and exaggeration of one's own and other religions, and must be abandoned. This involves even the claim that my religion is final, says Watt, and superior to all others. Essential to dialogue is listening, hearing what other religions have to say in the context of their own cultures. Then comes the 'acceptance of complementarity', admitting the fact that the great religions will continue to exist side by side for many decades to come, each being valid in its own sphere (Watt, *op. cit.*, 120-127).

The abandonment of the claim to finality and superiority will be disputed, though it explains Watt's own confession of being 'intellectually detached from both religions, while continuing to practise one' (p.v). This probably understates his belief in the divine activity in both Islam and Christianity, seeing that the Qur'ān comes from 'a divine initiative.' There is a parting of the ways between those who believe God to be at work in other religions, and those who see him in only one, or in none.

Listening to the Gītā may be congenial when it confirms beliefs that we already hold, as suggested above. But there are at least two further possibilities. A holy book may contradict our own scripture, or it may say something new and largely alien. When the Qur'ān declares that the Jews did not crucify Jesus (4.156), that seems a plain denial of a central fact of Christianity. Islam has accepted this denial in the past and has considered Christians to be in serious error. Yet modern study shows that the Quranic evidence is not simple : other verses suggest that the death of Jesus, and certainly the notion of a substitute crucified for Jesus, has no Quranic basis (see my *Jesus in the Qur'ān*). If there remains a clear division on the historicity of the crucifixion, that division must be recognized and this verse of the Qur'ān, taken baldly, cannot be the word of God to Christians. But while holding to what we believe to be true, and trying to make our own faith clear, we must try to understand what the Qur'ān really teaches and Muslims believe. The great Quranic and Islamic emphasis upon the will of God, apart from which no men could kill the Messiah, needs to be understood.

The Gītā, as pre-Christian, does not contradict facts of Christian history, but some of its doctrines might be thought irreconcilable with Christian faith. There seem to be two major forms of belief in immortality held among the religions : one thinks the soul is naturally immortal, and the other regards immortality as a gift bestowed by God. The Gītā believes in the eternal and indestructible nature of the soul, but while this is stated as in the non-theistic Sāṁkhya philosophy, and apparently the soul or many souls revolve continually in the endless round, yet the growing theism of the Gītā attaches them more and more to God. God himself is the life from which all beings spring, the soul in every being, the cause of beings, and the primal creator.

Certainly the Gītā's teaching on the soul is different from Christian doctrine if that is taken to imply that souls are created at birth and pass through only one earthly life, to end in bliss or in eternal torment. But the vagueness of much modern Christian teaching on immortality, and its neglect in preaching, has contributed to the widespread interest observable in Indian ideas of reincarnation. Yet the Bible itself, while presenting no consistent doctrine of the soul, speaks at the beginning of the breath of life or the spirit of God being breathed into man whereby he became a 'living soul' (Gen. 2.7), and at the end it tells of the redemption of souls and their reunion with the God from whom they derive all their being, when God shall be 'all in all' (1 Cor. 15,28). The Bible stresses, in different ways from the Gītā, the reality of sin that hides the divine spirit in man, and the purpose of both human life and the real world in which man is placed to do God's work. But it is likely that concepts of the nature of man and the world will be enriched in the West and in India by the cross-fertilization of these two great cultures.

The Gītā says some things that are new to Christian thought, but can they be claimed as words of God, even if they were unknown to the earthly Jesus? Modern theology admits the 'kenotic' limitations of the incarnation, and would regard it as absurd to suppose that Jesus knew or even anticipated the discoveries of modern science or biblical criticism. Similarly, religious teachings from that great stream of Indian revelation that is often different from the Semitic stream may be accepted, and may challenge us personally, bringing fresh light, if they are not contradictory to faith in Christ.

The Gītā is a book of Yoga, a word that has many meanings. In its teachings on meditation, on action detached from rewards, on knowledge and devotion, it has inspired many people in the West and can enlarge Christian horizons. Then the tolerance of much Indian religious life takes its pattern from the Gītā, and can be an example to the pugnacious West. Acceptance of the fact that men follow different ways, or even worship other gods, comes from seeing that all life is shot through with the presence of the divine.

Finally, the basic belief in the eternal soul may at least make us ponder more deeply on the nature of man than is customary in our modern world with its materialistic attitudes.

What the Gītā claims, and has been accepted as proving in the lives of countless men and women, is that God both speaks and acts. There is a word of God in every true statement and prayer: 'Whatever form a devotee seeks to worship with faith, it is I who ordain that unswerving faith' (7.21). There is also a special revelation: 'Hear my highest message, you are greatly beloved by me' (18.64). And there is divine action and appearance: 'Whenever righteousness appears to languish, I bring myself to birth' (4.7). In the Avatar event, in the teaching Guru, in the immanent and transcendent deity, the God of the Gītā has appeared true and living to Hindus, and he has produced an impact of truth upon more people beyond Hinduism today than ever before.

GEOFFREY PARRINDER is Professor of Study of Comparative Religions in the University of London. Author of *West African Religion*; *Religion in an African City*; *Introduction to Asian Religions*; *Comparative Religion*; *Worship in the World's Religions*; *Upanishads, Gītā and Bible*; *Jesus in the Qur'ān*; *Avator and Incarnation*; *The Bhagavad Gītā: a Verse Translation*, etc.

Islam and Incarnation

KENNETH CRAGG

It would seem naïve to ask whether the Christian's faith in the incarnation and 'the Word made flesh' separates him from the Muslim. For manifestly in history it does. Christology, as the New Testament, the Fathers, and the Church through the centuries have confessed it, has consistently found, and spelled, rejection on the part of Muslims – a rejection sanctified, apparently, by the explicit veto of the Qur'ān itself. The doctrine that is definitive of historic Christianity has met with the steady controversial repudiation of Muslims. The assumed hopelessness of the situation is well-known and it would seem pointless to explore it again.

These paragraphs, however, propose to do so by first rejecting the hopelessness and then venturing the question whether there cannot be (in the Muslim sense of the matter) a non-incarnational expression of Christian faith. Need the conviction of the divine in the human, as Christianity confesses it, incur the antipathy traditional to Muslim minds? The faith of the incarnation may, in fact and in tradition, sunder the two households. But *need* it do so? Or, in more positive terms, is there not a Christian sense of God in Christ truly compatible with the Islamic awareness of divine unity? And, conversely, is there not an Islamic sense of Christ compatible with the Christian understanding of divine self-revelation? Our starting point is that the answers in both cases can loyally be affirmative, however far from actuality in either case, and in popular form, the realization may be.

Clearly, on both sides, the actual answers are negative. But our concern, beyond these mutual strictures and cleavages, is with what is essential and potential, if we see the respective Islamic and Christian acknowledgements of God as open-ended and responsive to their own cognizances. And this is to be argued, not from some 'modern' or pragmatic compulsion (important as contemporary practicalities may be), but from the inner authenticity of their respective apprehension of the divine.

Nor is the discussion based, in any vital way, on the pleading of particular Quranic texts about 'Īsā (Jesus) as being 'a spirit from God,' and 'his word,' and 'a word from him.' Arguments that have been drawn in Christian quarters from these passages, suggesting that they intend more than might appear, are necessarily precarious and dubious, as long as we ignore the fundamental presuppositions of the Qur'ān about the divine relation to the human. Whatever may, or may not, be the historical and exegetical import of these verses, no case, from the Christian side, could rest securely on them, unless it rested also, and primarily, on an adequate reckoning with the whole consensus of Quranic witness about God and prophecy, with which their particular meaning is, of course, consistent. It will be sounder, in the end, to gather their implications into the larger issues upon which argument for a convergence of thought must rely.

Such issues, and such argument, have to do with what we must call the interpenetration of the divine and the human – as both faiths diversely confess it. The word 'sentness' is perhaps the best focus of this conviction, shared as it is by the two religions. 'He loved us and sent ...' the Christians say: 'He whom God hath sent,' said Jesus: 'to you is the word of this salvation sent,' said the apostles, preaching in Acts. There are, it is true, other verbs in the Christian vocabulary that describe this divine initiative, words such as 'gave' and 'came.' But let us defer, for the moment, the concord of these, in the simple recognition that 'sentness' fairly denotes what Christian acknowledgement of God in Christ believes.

Rasūl, the 'sent one,' is of course the fundamental definition of the prophet in Islam. *Rasūliyyah*, or 'mission from God' is the agency of the Qur'ān on earth. Such *Rasūliyyah* is culminatory, in the Islamic belief, of a sequence of divine address to the human situation, though a long succession of prophets and messengers, equipped with sacred 'pages' and with holy 'books,' intimating to their immediate constituencies of men, of lands, and peoples, the claims and commands of the heavenly will.

There is, doubtless a wide disparity between the religious elements and the instrumental factors in these many 'missions' to mankind, as well as in the biographical context and the historical occasions within which they ensued. It suffices here to centre attention on the human aegis and the divine fiat in every situation and to note the unmistakable interpenetration of the two, and, in that interpenetration, the real involvement of the divine in the temporal and the constant concern about the genuine mandate of the eternal. We will consider these aspects, first in respect of Quranic 'sentness,' and then in relation to Christ 'sentness,' and endeavour, in so doing, to illuminate a later discussion about their possible convergence in terms that remain 'incarnational' for the Christian, but continue 'non-incarnational' as the Muslims habitually suppose the 'incarnational' to be. Both the enterprise and its theological requirements of patience and clarity may claim to be an example of the task, if not also of the art, of religious dialogue and mutuality in our time.

The Quranic 'Association' of the Divine and the Human

'Association' is, of course, a dangerous word to venture here – or would be apart from the intimations of the previous paragraph. For 'association' is frequently the word used in English to translate the Arabic word *Shirk*, the cardinal sin of 'associating' the divine with the human, in the way that, for example, the idolaters do, when they imply divine abilities in their own creations. To divert from God alone to any such idol the attributes and the activities proper only to God most high is to be a *mushrik*, a committer of *Shirk*. *Islam* and the *muslim* are the utterly antithetical terms, repudiating in horror and zeal the distortions and perversities of the polytheists, whether they are literal or 'spiritual' idolaters, holding substitutes for God, and allowing these substitutes in their worship or their confidence or their anticipations of help. Against them all rings the emphatic *Lā ilāha illā Allāh.* 'Exalted be He above all that they associate.' For there is no god but God and there is none equal to Him.

It is precisely because of that undivided and inalienable sovereignty that revelation and prophecy must be understood as deriving only from his will and by his fiat. There cannot be other revealers, other ordainers, other arbiters, because 'there is none other God but He.' The source of prophethood is within the unity. Thus it is exactly that urgent and total 'dissociation' of God from idols, and from human representation therein, that involves and requires his authentic 'association' with human servants and with the human scene, in order that the meaning of His lordship may be obeyed and confessed among men. We might almost say that there *are* prophets *because* there *are not*, and should not be, idols. The mission of the former and the insistent non-entity of the latter are reciprocal demonstrations of the divine unity.

That very repudiation of idolatry takes us into the heart both of the Quranic 'mission' and of Islamic theology. For it requires us to contemplate the fact of idolatry as an aspect of humanity, to wrestle, that is, with the fact that this is the sort of world in which idolatry occurs, and to wrestle, therefore, with the further fact that the god Islam confesses is the sort of god within whose dominion idolatry could occur. To ponder this truth about God and our world – as we, both Muslim and Christians, too seldom do – is to be alerted to reflections very vital for us all.

It means that God has rights in man (for otherwise there is no point in law and prophecy enjoining them) and that man, being capable of idolatry, is able to withhold those rights to the ultimate degree. We are thus led to the recognition of a divine stake in man, of a divine 'interest' in his response. There is here, however un-congenial to traditional Islam, some element almost of divine 'vulnerability' in relation to man. Prophecy would not need to inveigh against idols if they were not inimical to the divine will, if they were not flouting a divine reign (*de facto*, of course, never *de jure*). The very iconcoclasm of Islam makes clear how crucial are the divine concerns in the human 'submission'. Certainly the divine authority is, by Quranic urgencies, deeply 'associated' with the human scene.

So much follows from this. It can hardly matter to God that we are idolaters, unless it matters that we *are*. Our being is significant to God at least as the point of the issue: *Shirk* or *Islam*? And of course it cannot be thus far significant, unless it is also significant much more. The very doctrines of creation and of providence, of revelation and of law, indicate a divine 'commitment', in the sense that we take them, to human existence. If we *are*, then God within creation is not unconditioned. For in his dealings with us there is a conditionality, in our frailty, in our mortality, in our sin and waywardness, in our capacity to refuse the word and take the idols. Criteria of divinity itself are manifestly at stake in these human issues. We might even speak, in this context, of a divine exposure to man. And that human scene, if read as addressed by law and shaped by creation, throws up in its long and tortured history many questions for the God of its lordship.

We cannot respond exclusively to God, as Islam directs, unless there is an essential divine relevance to the *whole* of that life from which our response must come. One cannot hold all things in and under God, as Islamic unity enjoins, if God himself is only partially related to history and to the world. A sole worship surely means an entire relevance of the One worshipped. The question, therefore, follows, what does divine adequacy entail?

That we are here in the midst of characteristically Christian instincts of mind does not reduce their Islamic significance. We are only taking Islamic lordship in its own seriousness.

To do so is to leave no place for the suggestion that the divine 'vulnerability' to human recalcitrance and perversity is in fact no 'vulnerability,' because divine sovereignty somehow 'arranges' the human hostility, which would cease immediately did the inscrutable will of heaven so decree. The concern for omnipotence implicit in this crudity distorts omnipotence itself. Empty of any comprehensible reckoning with the realization of sovereignty, it has no merit or authenticity, and it rides ill with the urgency of Muslim prophecy. If we end with a kind of puppet-show of the moral world we have certainly departed from the eloquent sincerity of Islamic worship.

Neither is there escape from the 'association' of divine 'interests' with human conditions of their achievement by scouting, as some Muslim theologians have done, the whole conviction of divine relation to the world other than in the imperatives of law. For these inevitably involve the nature whence they derive. We can, if we like, think God out of relation, as it were, with the 'subjunctives' of our life, in an emphasis merely on His 'imperatives,' and thus withhold ourselves from any thoughts of a divine accountability to our situation. But how meagrely this is to conceive the sovereignty! Some, it is true, in Islamic philosophy, have set the divine sovereignty in such unquestionability that no aspirations or interrogatives can ever be addressed to it. God then emerges as a being who allows men no 'rights' before Him and no areas of experience about which they can say: 'He will,' or 'He ought.' Then there is nothing that God *must* be in relation to men. He *may* be just, merciful, compassionate, but only and always by fiat of untrammelled will, never by pledge of essential nature. Such an unpredictability in God must be distinguished from the simple, and worthy, feeling that definition is limitation, or from a laudable diffidence about speculation. When it is held as an existential 'vacuity' of the divine nature, it imperils the whole moral and prophetic essence of Islam and excludes anything conceivably religious. That 'there is no god but God' can never be translated into the implication: 'There is no God, only "x".' For the latter neither needs nor possesses any repudiations.

Returning, then, from these evasions, to the reality of the divine 'association' in the human, we reach the other central factor in our reflections, namely the relation of the human/prophetic to the divine. 'Sentness', as we saw, presupposes a human aegis for divine purposes. There is that significant *waṣlah*, or link, in the Islamic *Shahādah*, or confession of faith, between Allāh and Muḥammad. It is there also in the large round discs in the mosques bearing the two terms that denote God *and* his messenger. 'God and ...' There is the charisma of the human agency to serve and effectuate the divine will. What is 'from' God is thereby 'through' the Prophet, and so 'for' the human constituency which the Prophet addresses in the divine behalf.

There are two crucial elements in that instrumentality, namely its human reality and its indubitable commission. We shall find both of these figuring, with equal centrality, in the Christian conviction of the incarnation. But, postponing that reflection, we notice how the Islamic non-incarnational understanding of Muḥammad involves certain congruent necessities. The Prophet 'has' the divine mandate and in some sense it engages and energizes his whole person and biography. The Qur'ān impinges on the sequences of a career in its vocation. The content of the book and the unfolding of prophethood are parallel realities. There is no space here to explore the nature of Muḥammad's charisma in its Quranic setting. The sufficient fact is his 'association' in the Islamic mind with the word from heaven, as recipient and speaker. All the authority of the Scripture flows from the 'guaranteedness' of that 'association'. There is need for this to be inviolate and indubitable. *Kitāb lā raiba fīhi* – 'a book in which there is no dubiety'. The phenomenon of the Qur'ān is thus inseparable from what we may call the phenomenon of Muḥammad and both may be seen as a supreme expression of humanness instrumental to God.

This, of course, is steadily emphasized throughout Islamic history and theology. The Prophet is only a man, but superlatively so, because through him there has occurred the *Tanzīl*, which has communicated the will of heaven to men on earth. It is for sublimely transcendental reasons that, in Islam, this instrumentality has been understood and interpreted always short of 'divinity'.[1] Yet the instrumentality is crucial and involves deeply human qualities in a mystery of 'afflatus', of eloquence, of tenacity under hostility, and of psychic energy and soul-force. The Qur'ān, as divine word, is intensely a human phenomenon, and takes its place vitally in human history.

In insisting that the Prophet is 'only' a prophet, Islam and the

Qur'ān surely mean us to understand, not that there is some
fragility or dubiety in the revelation, but that it is incontestably
'divine.' The 'only,' here, does not derogate the agency: it exalts
the source. The concern (which is exactly that, as we must see, of
Christian doctrine in relation to the incarnation) is for the status
of the revelation. The purpose is to ensure the priority, the initiative, of the source of the sentness. If the sentness is to be inviolate
(i.e. authoritative) the source must be inviolable. It is, we may say,
because Muḥammad is sent from the divine that he is emphatically
human. The status of prophet is identified in human texture that it
may be known to be authoritatively God's doing. Need there be
sundering controversy, or necessary alienation, if another household
of faith should see the same inviolability of origin and authorative-
ness of means assured by these very criteria in another dimension?
This brings us to the Christian sphere, where the same desire to be
able to say: 'This is *from* God and *for* God ...' lives by the
conviction that says: 'This *is* God *with* us.' There is again the
human locus and there is the divine source. The difference lies in
how we conceive them to be coactive.[2]

The Christ 'Association' of the Divine and the Human

Though Islam is historically subsequent to Christianity, can we
not say that in all the foregoing we have a kind of paradigm into
which, from a sufficient (though in no sense a total) identity of
conviction, we could fit the Christian scheme, provided we are
ready to enlarge the criteria of what a human aegis, serving a
divine purpose in the human situation, would involve? At least,
the same suppositions are there – divine sovereignty, the human
realm created and governed from heaven, the fact of law and
mercy, the seriousness of history, and the role of the human/
prophetic within it. The Christian gospel certainly holds these
same convictions within its own uniqueness. It understands God
as related to the world in the sovereignty of law and in the embassies
of prophets.

Creation, law, providence and revelation, in their Christian
'incidence,' derive from their Old Testament antecedents a much
livelier, unreluctant sense of the human claim on God and the
divine stake in man. But it is important not to let that large difference obscure the common fact of the 'association' we are arguing.
Those Old Testament categories are, of course, vastly revolutionized
in their human range, breaking out of ethnic separatism into

universal reach. They are also deeply transformed in their divine criteria so that, in Messiahship according to Jesus, the divine solicitude for men undertakes in suffering the whole cost of their redemption. Vulnerability there becomes the ultimate clue to power itself. We have the same Old Testament conviction that man's apprehension of God is in the texture of events themselves. But what those events are, in ministry, cross, grave, and resurrection, moves eloquently from the privacy and self-centredness of exodus and the perplexity of exile into the saving discovery of messianic achievement in Christ according to Jesus, crucified and risen.

There is a striking passage in Isa. 52.6, by which we may express its meaning:

> This is why my people shall know my Name: on that day they shall understand that it is I who say: 'Behold I am here'.

'It is I who say: "Behold I am here."' *Ego qui loquebar, ecce adsum*, God in His own recognizances, determining and giving the criteria by which He is disclosed, God being known to men in manhood itself. In this incarnate Word, the Christian faith identifies both a human aegis and a divine activity, but sees them conjoined, by virtue of what either is to the other – by virtue, that is, of what the conjoining accomplishes in the human and conveys of the divine. The whole is, as it were, a divine autograph, signed in the fabric of definitive experience at the heart of elemental issues in human living, having to do with truth and justice, power and mercy, love and suffering, life and death. Here the vulnerability in God, which law somehow assumes by its very claims, and which iconoclasm means to obviate utterly by its energy against idols, is seen – accepted and transformed – at the very heart of an inclusive drama that effectuates, against all idolatry, the redemptive victory of God.

Is this really a different world of discourse from the Islamic? In criteria of both divine and human things in their feasible 'association,' doubtless yes! But, in the heart of conviction, that God reigns against all challenge, and reigns through human 'sentness,' surely no! This Christian, incarnational self-revelation of the divine, through event and apprehension in the human, is firmly within that sovereignty and unity in which Islam believes. It has also vitally to do with the undoing of idolatry. There is the same 'sentness', *qua* divine initiative, *qua* human aegis. The 'coming' from God is certainly more than a commissioning for Him. But if the mission means the very Presence, it is still 'mission' out of sovereignty, engaging human personality in its purpose.

Is it only our lack of adventure in spiritual relationship that makes us loath to explore the kindredness here that has to do with the instrumentality to God, prophetic and incarnational? Or is it that we are simply daunted by the controversial distance we accept between them? Islamic minds have been traditionally reluctant to think that the divine 'association' with human instrumentality could ever go beyond the prophetic. It is still not reassured that the care for unity can well abandon this reluctance. There is also the instinct that feels that the more something is God's the less it is man's. The 'miracle' is greater if the prophet is 'illiterate'. Christian commitment to the incarnation, for its part, queries and worries if uniqueness seems to be imperilled by any sense of continuity between what happens in prophecy and what happens in Christ.

Yet on either side, these loyalties to dogma need not seem, or stay, so adamant or aloof, if we take them in their own seriousness and interrelation. It is surely clear, as we have argued, from the Qur'ān, that Muḥammad's prophethood, far from being a cypher or a 'vacuity' of mind and person, is a profound 'association' of personal involvement and divine 'authorization'. Christian faith in the incarnate Word, for its part, has to know that the paradox of the divine-human, which it there confesses, belongs, however remotely, with all occasions of law, providence, prophecy, and revelation. For every instance of human charisma in divine employ, every coinciding of historical event with heavenly intent, contains in its own measure, this mystery of the eternal and the temporal at rendezvous. To believe in the incarnation is not to exclusify that mystery. For it is relatively present everywhere in creation and without it this could not be the sort of world in which *the* incarnation could happen.

Christians, it is true, have often been slow to allow this sense in which all prophecy and all revelation are 'incarnational' in that they locate what God is saying in what men are and do. Yet the Christian meaning of God-in-Christ surely illuminates all human instrumentality to God, albeit with an intensity and an ultimacy wholly its own. Thus we have the paradox of it, in the gospel, not dark, opaque, and tentative, to be shelved as a problem, but luminous and central as a clue to all else.[3] In such temper the Christian faith readily accepts the intimations elsewhere of what it sees consummated in Christ. It keeps its doctrine of God in Christ properly continuous with its related doctrine of the Holy Spirit. For there also it reads the same paradox of the purpose and presence of the divine within the 'grieving,' broken yet also glorious, relatedness of the human scene.

In all this, the concern of the Chalcedonian, and other formulations of Christian orthodoxy about the incarnation, with all the liabilities of their Greek context of discourse, must be seen as a true and instinctive solicitude for the authenticity of the divine character of the revelation. There is here, in Christian terms, the same will to assurance of the divine imprimatur which, in Islamic terms, makes for the status of Muḥammad as 'the messenger,' and of the Qur'ān to which he is instrumental as the divinely preserved and mediated word. The human has to be known in its divine credentials: the divine must be authenticated in its human locus. Traditional minds, in either faith, may see this common issue of the 'rightness' of association as infinitely disparate and contrasted. The present case is that, in 'association' itself, in 'sentness' with its divine fiat and its human aegis, we have a potentially recognizable affinity, beyond and beneath all else, however abiding and exacting the disparities.

But if we can argue a sympathy from Islamic criteria for the Christ 'association' of God with the world and from Christian criteria for the Quranic 'sentness' from God to the world, is not everything jeopardized by the overriding condition of the divine greatness? *Allāhu akbar.*

Yet is this an unambiguous matter, a conclusive veto, a closed anathema? Certainly the Islamic concern for the divine majesty seems to preclude the Christian interpretation of Christ and God. Indeed it might look like a *tour de force*, ingenious perhaps but certainly hopeless, to suppose that this Christian account of incarnation could ever be Islamically possible. But is this really the whole story?

At least there is here no deification. Christian faith about Jesus is not 'incarnational' in any Graeco-Roman, 'pantheonic' sense, where the ranks of divinity are supposedly recruited from the famous of the earth. The direction of conviction is all the other way, not the assertion of divinization *post facto*, but the recognition of the divine *a priori*. If we may ignore calendar time, we say that the Church of the New Testament and beyond had a zealously Islamic passion for the divine unity. Hence their veto, courageously, on Caesar worship, and their sturdy insistence on the inalienability of the divine lordship. They were thoroughly Muslim folk in their jealousy for God alone. The effect of their preaching was a lively dethronement of the idols. Their making room for Christ within their experience of God was to deepen, not to endanger, its exclusive authority. They saw that experience as the culmination of their Hebraic (and, again anachronistically, their Islamic) conviction that events on the empirical plane could be the point of convergence of divine providence and truth. So they dared to recognize what they understood as such a convergence, to them final, and inclusive. Their only right response was worship. Anything less would have failed to acknowledge the presence they had known.

Nor did they fear that in so worshipping they had discounted the majesty on high or brought into their responsive thought of God a dimension inconsistent with His unity and glory. Quite the contrary. They felt themselves proceeding upon new and glorious criteria of that by which God was God indeed. Their convictions about Christ were wholly in the context of their convictions about God. Both were authentic by that very mutuality. For this, con- cretely, was the meaning of the incarnation. 'Believe in God', 'believe in me,' (John 14.1), were reciprocal imperatives – and affirmatives.

It is sometimes conjectured that the incarnation would be less intolerable if it were more splendid. Shepherds, for example, make a very lowly analogy for omnipotence. Emirs might do much better. But we do not arrive at what might be 'adequate' for God by criteria of rank, or size, or notions of competitive status among ourselves. 'Exalted be He above *all* that they associate.' The criteria of divine greatness cannot well be those of our devising or requiring. It takes God to show us what they are. But we may expect them to be those of a faithful creator and of the lord of history. Truly the vision of the divine glory recognizable in the strong arms stretched upon a cross of pain, embracing the world that had rejected him, was a disconcerting measure of the divine reality. But if we hold on together to the common clue, vital to us both, of human-divine inter-relevance, then it is possible to understand how this might truly be the pattern of a divine power effectively master of the human world.

Deliberately, thus far, we have not spoken of 'sonship'. For it is urgent we should ponder the issues away from the tyranny, if such it be, of battlefield vocabulary. Part of the duty of comparative theology is the art of adequate paraphrase. We only rightly possess our terminology in the capacity to do without it. Otherwise, our thinking is crutch-ridden and does not move in freedom. It will always be true that for Christians 'Father and Son' are terms hallowed and prescribed by scriptural warrant and authority. They have therefore a vital role. Yet our very receiving of them thus needs the living loyalty that is able to confess them alternatively. This is the more so where, as with Islam, they are essentially misconstrued and seem irretrievably provocative.[4]

What then do we mean when we say that God is 'the Father of our Lord Jesus Christ,' and that 'Jesus is the Son of God'? What will be our adequately Christian and intelligibly Muslim paraphrase?

Do we not mean that transcendent reality, bearing sovereign responsibility for the world, undertakes within the inner quality of that sovereignty and in self-consistency the initiatives of grace and truth which we identify, by their own light, in the credentials actively verified in the Christ of what we call the gospel? We mean that the power within creation and behind history discloses itself to us, out of its own freedom, in terms original to its own glory and realized in human personality within an encounter of word and deed, central to the whole mystery and tragedy of our human being as we know it in our hearts. 'Begets,' 'sends,' 'gives,' are all, in their meaning, translations of this fact. That 'the Father sends the Son ...' that 'God so loved that He gave ...' that 'the only begotten ... in the bosom of the Father has declared Him ...' say this in affirming, analogically, the impulse whence and the likeness wherewith the revelation comes. The impulse and the likeness cannot be separated. For they are the same self-consistency in the eternal and the temporal. And, if we are tempted to question whether 'initiative' can ever 'happen' in the eternal or ever 'occur' in the temporal, the answer will be that the questioners themselves would not exist outside the 'happening' they interrogate. The paradox of speaking of 'God *and* His messenger,' or of 'God *and* Christ' is one already with the paradox that speaks of 'God *and* the world.' It is 'the God with Whom we have to do' in being human, who has to do with us in being divine. We believe we are recognizing our humanity as it is, when we confess that relatedness. Where we differ is in understanding and confessing how the fabric of our human experience receives and recognizes the divine relatedness. Of the common fact of it there is no doubt. It is the very greatness of God that it should be so.

Perhaps in the end, through all the controversies we have here ignored, there emerges this conjecture: was it Islam's calling to guard the fact of that greatness and the Christians' to cherish humanly how great it is?

NOTES

1 Popular religion in Islam, both Sunnī and Shī'ah, has not always uniformly or readily conformed to this understanding, but has developed forms of devotion to the Prophet's person and celebrations of his birth (*maulids*) inconsistent with the strictness of theology – witness the zeal of the Wahhābī movement, for example, in their suppression. The Quranic phrase *Ṣallā Allāhu 'alaihi wa sallam* ('God salute and greet him with peace') has often been interpreted in a sense that has divinity greeting itself in his humanity. But such 'hypostasising,' though often vigorous, is properly heretical.

2 It is significant, in this same connection, that comparable discussions arise in Islamic and Christian theology about the 'eternity' of the Qur'ān on the one hand, and the pre-existence of Christ on the other.

3 Perhaps the best exposition of this 'continuity' of the incarnation with creation and history is that of Donald Baillie, *God was in Christ* (1948). In *Prospect for Theology* (1967), pp. 139-66, John Hick in 'Christology at the Crossroads', is at pains to question this continuity, and insists that 'the Incarnation is an all-or-nothing event ...' But while some of his criticisms of the 'process theology' language may be justified, his own 'scientific' attempt to escape from the Chalcedonian Christology, while yet defending it, leaves the impression that he ought to look again more critically at his basic interpretation. We must beware of ending with the kind of world in which the incarnation is no longer a truth about our humanity as well as about the Christ we say indwells it.

4 It is useful to recall here that what repeatedly the Qur'ān disavows in its references to Jesus and 'divinity' is not the Christian doctrine of the incarnation, but the Christian heresy of adoptionism. The recurrent term is *ittakhadha*, with the sense of 'to take to oneself' and *walad* ('a son') as object! 'Far be it from the eternal to take unto Himself a son' (e.g. Sūrah 19.35, Cf.19.92 and 25.2). There is no doubt that the Qur'ān intends to repudiate the whole Christian theme of God incarnate and the words 'God resist them: how they are perverse!' (9.30) are directed in imprecation against Christians, among others, because they hold that 'Messiah is the son of God.' Yet adoptionism is broadly what it has in mind. It is possible in

this way to relieve the orthodox Christian faith of much of the burden of explicit Quranic repudiation. See a fuller discussion in the appendix to R. C. Zaehner's *At Sundry Times* (1958).

KENNETH CRAGG is Assistant Bishop (Anglican) in the Middle East and Reader in Religious Studies, University of Sussex. Author of *The Call of the Minaret*; *Sandals at the Mosque*; *The Dome and the Rock*; *Counsels in Contemporary Islam*; *Christianity in World Perspective*; *The House of Islam*; *Alive to God*; *The Event of the Qur'ān, etc.*

The Outcome: Dialogue into Truth

JOHN HICK

Our conference was originally convened to investigate 'the relation-ship between world religions, especially in view of their apparently conflicting truth claims'. And this was in the event the dominating topic of our conversation. Some of the papers and much of the discussion dealt explicitly with the question of whether there is indeed a problem of conflicting truth claims; and others, assuming that there is such a problem, began the move that must then be attempted through it and beyond it.

The 'conflicting truth claims' problem is just that the different religions seem to say different and incompatible things about the nature of ultimate reality, about the modes of divine activity, and about the nature and destiny of man. Is the divine nature personal or non-personal? Does deity become incarnate in the world? Are human beings born again and again on earth? Is the Bible, or the Qur'ān, or the Bhagavad-Gītā the word of God? If what Christianity says in answer to these questions is true, must not what Hinduism says be to a large extent false? If what Buddhism says is true, must not what Islam says be largely false? This is the problem with which we began.

However there were those, especially Wilfred Cantwell Smith, who maintained that this was a false problem, and that a right understanding of the different faiths of different men must begin with a systematic dismantling of this unreal dilemma.

In his very important book *The Meaning and End of Religion*[1], Cantwell Smith had already challenged the familiar concept of 'a religion', on which part at least of the traditional problem of conflicting truth claims rests. He there emphasizes that what we call a religion, as an empirical entity that can be traced historically and mapped geographically, is a human phenomenon. Christianity, Hinduism, Judaism, Buddhism, Islam, and so on are human crea-tions whose history is part of the wider history of human culture. In his book Cantwell Smith traces the development of the concept of a religion as a distinct and bounded historical phenomenon and shows that the notion, so far from being universal and self-evident, is a distinctively Western invention that has been exported to the rest of the world. 'It is', he says, summarizing the upshot of his detailed historical argument, 'a surprisingly modern aberration for anyone to think that Christianity is true or that Islam is – since the Enlightenment, basically, when Europe began to postulate religions as intellectualistic systems, patterns of doctrines, so that they could for the first time be labelled "Christianity" and "Buddhism", and could be called true or false'.[2] This notion of religions as mutually exclusive entities with their own characteristics and histories, although it now tends to operate as a habitual category of our thinking, may well be but another example of the illicit reification, the turning of good adjectives into bad substantives, to which the Western mind is prone and against which contemporary philosophy has warned us. In this case a powerful but false conceptuality has helped to create phenomena answering to it, namely the religions of the world seeing themselves and each other as rival ideological communities.

Perhaps however, instead of thinking of religion as existing in mutually exclusive systems, we should see the religious life of mankind as a dynamic continuum within which certain major disturbances have from time to time set up new fields of force, of greater or lesser extent, displaying complex relationships of attraction and repulsion, absorption, resistance, and reinforcement. These major disturbances are the great creative religious moments of human history from which the distinguishable religious traditions have stemmed. Theologically, such moments are intersections of divine grace, divine initiative, divine truth, with human faith, human response, human enlightenment. They have made their impact upon the stream of human life so as to affect the development of cultures; and Christianity, Islam, Hinduism, Buddhism are among the resulting historical-cultural phenomenon. It is clear, for example, that Christianity has developed through a complex interaction between religious and non-religious factors. Christian ideas have been formed within the intellectual framework provided by Greek philosophy; the Christian church was moulded as an institution by the Roman empire and its system of laws; the Catholic mind reflects something of the Latin Mediterranean temperament and the Protestant mind something of the northern Germanic temperament; and so on. It is not hard to appreciate the connections between historical Christianity and the continuing life of man in the western hemisphere; and of course just the same is true in their own ways of all the other religions in the world.

This means that it is not appropriate to speak of a religion as being true or false, any more than it is to speak of a civilization as being true or false. For the religions, in the sense of distinguishable religio-cultural streams within man's history, are expressions of the diversities of human types and temperaments and thought forms. The same differences between the eastern and western minds that are revealed in different conceptual and linguistic, social, political and artistic forms, presumably also underlie the contrasts between eastern and western religion.

In *The Meaning and End of Religion* Cantwell Smith examines the development from the original religious event or idea, whether it be the insight of the Buddha, or the life of Christ, or the career of Muḥammad, to a religion in the sense of a vast living organism with its own credal backbone and its institutional skin. And he shows in each case that this development stands in a questionable relationship to that original event or idea. Religions as institutions, with the theological doctrines and the codes of behaviour that form their boundaries, did not come about because the religious reality required this but because such a development was historically virtually inevitable in the days of undeveloped communication between the different cultural groups. But now that the world has become a communicational unity we are moving into a new situation in which it becomes proper for religious thinking to transcend these cultural-historical boundaries. Instead of asking, Which religion is true – Christianity, or Hinduism, or Islam ... ? we can see these religions as historic streams of human life, each of which may be built partly upon truth and partly upon error. Instead then of asking whether a religion, as such, is true in some absolute sense we are free to recognize religious truth, wherever it is evident, within all man's cultures and civilizations.

Cantwell Smith summarizes the conclusions of *The Meaning and End of Religion* as follows: 'What men have tended to conceive as religion and especially as a religion, can more rewardingly, more truly, be conceived in terms of two factors, different in kind, both dynamic: an historical "cumulative tradition", and the personal faith of men and women' (p. 175). And the *locus* of religious truth, he goes on to argue in *Questions of Religious Truth*, is the latter element, the personal faith of individuals. It is, he says, 'dangerous and impious to suppose that Christianity is true, as an abstract system, something "out there" impersonally subsisting, with which we can take some comfort in being linked – its effortless truth justifying us, and giving us status. Christianity, I would suggest, is not true absolutely, impersonally, statically; rather it can *become* true, if and as you or I appropriate it to ourselves and interiorize it, insofar as we live it out from day to day. It becomes true as we take it off the shelf and personalize it, in dynamic actual existence' (pp. 67-8). One effect of this new approach is to transform the traditional question of conflicting religious truth claims. It has transformed that question – but it has not dissolved it away. Religions as complex historical phenomena, we can see, are not true or false; but nevertheless particular religious ideas, affirmations, teachings, beliefs, doctrines, dogmas, theories are presumably still true or false – if not absolutely then at least comparatively. To take an example that figured in our discussions, the doctrine of reincarnation looks as though it must be either true of false. As between two people, one of whom asserts reincarnation while the other denies it, it seems that one must be – to say the least – much more nearly right than the other. Likewise, as between one who asserts the personal and the other impersonal character of the ultimate divine reality. Or the unity and the triunity of God. Or the divinity and the non-divinity of Christ.

And so in his paper on 'A Human View of Truth', together with his book *Questions of Religious Truth*, which we discussed at the conference together with the paper, Wilfred Cantwell Smith seeks to take his dissolution of the 'problem of conflicting religious truth claims' a stage further. In these writings he puts forward two theses that fit together and support one another. The main thesis of *Questions of Religious Truth* is that 'religions' are not in themselves true or false but that a religion may *become* true in the life of a man of faith who is related to God within the historical context of that religion. And the main thesis of the article is that truth is not only the correspondence of propositions with reality, but also, and even more importantly so far as religious truth is concerned, integrity and faithfulness in a person. The connection between the two theses (if I understand them rightly) is that the sense in which a religion can become true within the life of the faithful is this latter sense, which Cantwell Smith calls the personalistic sense of 'truth'.

Cantwell Smith is, it would seem, saying that the fundamental notion expressed by the word 'truth' is right relationship to reality. The right relationship of an indicative proposition to reality is that of accurately describing some aspect or fragment of reality. Personal truth, or truth in the sense in which it is located in a person, on the other hand, is to be found in his will, his intention, his desire, the orientation of his mind, and in the consequent style and quality of his life. It consists in his desire and intention to relate himself rightly to reality. This means in practice an openness to reality and a sincere living out of such knowledge as he has.

Now Cantwell Smith makes it entirely clear that he is not for a moment denying either the propriety or the importance of the notion of propositional truth, but rather emphasizing the immense importance of the more neglected idea of personalistic truth – though I am inclined to prefer a descriptive (and metaphorical) phrase for it, such as 'the moral truthfulness of a person's life'. And so his emphasis at this point is not very different, if at all different, from that of those in all traditions who have insisted that we are to be doers and not merely hearers of the word; that it is the faith expressed in our actions that matters; that truth – particularly moral and religious truth – must become existential, so that as well as thinking it we feel it and respond to it and live by it. In Cardinal Newman's terminology, it must be real and not merely notional. One familiar writer who is full of this emphasis is the Christian mystic, Thomas à Kempis, who again and again says things like this: 'Truly, at the day of judgement we shall not be examined as to what we have read, but as to what we have done; not as to how well we have spoken, but as to how religiously we have lived'.[3] The novelty of Cantwell Smith's article is in his detailed philological investigation showing that this personalistic conception of truth has always been central to Islamic thinking and, more importantly still, in the suggestion that in seeing religious truth as primarily personalistic rather than propositional we dissolve the supposed problem of conflicting religious truth claims.

In support of this thesis Cantwell Smith reminds us that religion is concerned, not primarily with ideas and propositions, but with life itself – with the concrete character and quality of our experience and activity, embodying our faith-response to God. His thesis rests, he says, 'on the quiet, but firm, basis that true religion is a quality of personal living; that whatever else it be, religious life is a kind of life. It is a relation – a living relation – between man and God; an actual relation, new every morning, between particular, real men, in concrete, changing situations, and God'.[4] He likewise reminds us, as part of the same emphasis, that divine revelation, as communication from God to man, can only be said to have taken place when it has been received by man responding in faith to the divine initiative. And just as revelation is only real or actual in so far as it *becomes* so by being responded to, so more generally religion, as man's relationship to God, is only real, or authentic, or true, by *becoming* so in the person and life of the religious man. In other words, religion consists in an actual lived relationship to God, and not in the holding of beliefs, even though they be true beliefs, about God.

Now 'Christianity', 'Islam', 'Hinduism' and so on – these being terms that Cantwell Smith is only willing to use within inverted commas – are different historical contexts within which men have lived, and failed to live, in relationship to God. Such living in relationship to God is a matter of degree: for faith can wax and wane, decay and develop, grow and collapse. And so far as a man does live in faith, or does live in relationship to God, within the context of a given 'religion', and in terms of its tradition of belief and practice, to that extent 'religion' has become true in his life.

Thus Cantwell Smith says of 'Christianity' that it 'is not true absolutely, impersonally, statically: rather, it can *become* true, if and as you and I appropriate it to ourselves and interiorize it, insofar as we live it out from day to day'.[5] Again, speaking now not only of 'Christianity' but of any religion, he says: 'A devout person, whose sense of the presence of God is both vivid and sincere, and of his own unworthiness as he bows in that presence, may plead for God's mercy, and humbly know the quiet transport of its assurance because of his personal and living faith that God is indeed merciful. At that moment the truth of that man's religiousness is perhaps a different matter from the question of the earthly path by which he arrived at his awareness and his faith, or of the community of which he is a member. The truth of his religion in its actual, living quality – the private, personal religion that is really and significantly *his* – is a different question from, and again I would say a more interesting question to God himself, as well as to you and me, than any question of the truth or otherwise of "his religion" in the abstract, formal, systematic sense of the religion of his historical community generally'.[6]

All this seems to me to be both true and important. But nevertheless I want to argue that it does not get us 'off the hook' of the problem of the relation between the truth-claims of the different religions that become true in the lives of their sincere adherents. For surely 'Christianity' or 'Islam' or 'Hinduism' can only *become* true in the personalistic sense because they are already true in another, more universal and objective though less existential sense. Just as revelation is only real when it is responded to, but on the other hand can only be responded to because it is already 'there' to be responded to, so a religion, as an historical context consisting of religious beliefs and practices, can only become personalistically true in a man's life because those beliefs were already true beliefs, pointing towards and not away from the divine reality, and because those practices were already appropriate rather than inappropriate as ways in which to worship and serve the divine reality.

This can be expressed more concretely in terms of an incident which Cantwell Smith relates in his book. 'Once I was climbing in the Himalayas, not far from a settlement but along a track somewhat remote, and came across a fruit seller, a humble and poor and lovable old man with a stack of oranges that he was selling by weight, so many *annas* per *sir*, or we might say so many cents per pound. For scales he had a rough-and-ready balance, consisting of two pans suspended by strings attached at each end of a rough crossbar. The bar he held in his hand suspended by a string from its mid-point. He put oranges in one pan and weighed them against some rocks he had there, a middle-sized one and two smallish ones the three of which together made up one *sir* (two pounds). He was too poor to own metal weights, stamped and standard. That the three stones actually weighed a *sir* was an unverified presumption; though I personally believe that they did. I watched him a while, as he made occasional sales to passers-by; and afterwards fell into conversation with him. He was far from any possibility of having his dealings checked; and there was no external measure of his honesty, which I found was sustained rather by a verse from the Qur'ān which runs "Lo! He over all things is watching". Now because he believed the Qur'ān to be the word of God, that verse ringing in his ears from memory signified to him that God Himself was watching him and was telling him to be honest. Now I submit that in that situation, God was in fact that particular afternoon speaking to that particular shrivelled old man in the words of the Qur'ān – or through the words of the Qur'ān, if you prefer'.[7] And Cantwell Smith draws this conclusion, 'Might we say that the statement "the Qur'ān is the Word of God", rather than being in itself true or false, at a generic or abstract level, impersonally, can become true – in the life of a particular person; many persons; and further, that it has become more true in the lives of certain persons, at certain times, than others. It becomes true through faith'.[8]

There is here a convincing religious insight. But is there not also an unnecessary and confusing divorce between personalistic and propositional truth? To say that in the old orange-seller's life on that particular day the Islamic religion 'became true' is, surely, to presuppose that it was and is true that Allah is real and is aware of all that is taking place in our human world. We would not be willing to say that Islam has become true in this man's life if we were not also willing to say that what he believes – namely, the reality and righteousness and all-seeingness of Allah – is also true. The idea of a religion's becoming true in a devout man's life presupposes, it seems to me, the idea of that religion's already being true in the sense of resting on true assertions, or perhaps true presuppositions, concerning 'what there is' and 'how things are'.

Putting this again, negatively, I hope that Cantwell Smith is not saying that the truth of a 'religion' or of faith consists simply in the fact that it 'works', producing good fruits in human life, even if its basic associated beliefs should be false. For he could be read, or misread, as entirely separating personalistic truth from propositional truth and saying that the truth of a 'religion' consists wholly in its being sincerely practised and not at all in the universe being as the discourse of that religion presumes it to be. But if he is not saying this, then the problem, or at least the prima facie problem, of the conflicting truth claims of different religions remains with us.

To define the issue as sharply as possible let me raise the question whether there is any difference between saying of someone 'He is a true Christian (or Muslim or Hindu)', and saying 'Christianity (or Islam or Hinduism) has become true in his life'? There seem to be two possible answers to this question, namely yes and no.

If no, if there is no difference, so that for Christianity to be true is just for there to be true Christians, then it seems to follow that Christianity could be true even if there were no God, and Christ is not the 'Son of God', and men are not made in the image of God for fellowship with God. In other words, the central Christian affirmations could be false, and yet Christianity be true in that there are true Christians, people who sincerely and truly live out the Christian faith. To say that the Christian faith is true would then simply be to say that there are sincere people whose faith it is. It would not be to affirm more than that Christianity is believed and lived.

But in this purely personalistic and subjective sense Nazism was also a true faith, as is warlock worship, and faith in witchcraft and in astrology. To say that whatever is sincerely believed and practised is, by definition, true, would be the end of all critical discrimination, both intellectual and moral. Surely, then, the truth of a faith or of a religion cannot be reduced to the fact that someone sincerely believes it and lives on the basis of it. Surely we must insist that religion involves knowledge of God as well as a way of life. To be sure, the knowledge is no good without the life, but merely a clanging gong or a tinkling cymbal; and in so far as Cantwell Smith is emphasizing this, we must all agree with him. But equally the life is no good if the 'knowledge' on which it is based is not knowledge at all but delusion.

The other possible answer to the question I posed is yes. In that case the truth of Christianity (or Islam or Hinduism) does not consist without remainder in there being true Christians (or Muslims, or Hindus). In addition to this it consists, presumably, in the reality, or authenticity, of the knowledge of God which occurs in Christianity, or Islam, or Hinduism. But in that case we still have with us the problem of the at least apparently conflicting truth-claims of different religions. If Christianity cannot become (personalistically) true in a man's life unless it is (propositionally) true that God, as depicted in the New Testament, is real, and that Jesus is God's love incarnate; and if, again, Islam cannot become (personalistically) true in a man's life unless it is (propositionally) true that God, as depicted in the Qur'ān, is real and that God does not become incarnate; and if, again, Vedāntic Hinduism cannot become (personalistically) true in a man's life unless it is (propositionally) true that the ultimate reality, Brahman, is non-personal and only mythologically to be described as personal love; and if yet again, Theravāda Buddhism can only become (personalistically) true in a man's life if it is (propositionally) true that there is no God and no continuing human soul – then in order to affirm that all these different faiths can become (personalistically) true in the lives of their sincere adherents it seems that we must be able to affirm that all their essential (propositional) beliefs are true. But how can it be true both that there is and that there is not a personal God; both that Christ is God incarnate, and that God does not become incarnate? This is the problem of the conflicting, or at least apparently conflicting truth claims of different religions; and this problem is not dissolved by Wilfred Cantwell Smith's otherwise extremely illuminating and valuable new way of seeing religion and religions.

It seemed to me however that our conference discussions offered hints – though no more than hints – of another approach, and one which may prove to be a path along which progress can be made; and I should like to end by trying to point to the beginnings of this path.

This approach presupposes a distinction between, on the one hand, man's encounters, in the various forms of religious experience, with the divine reality and, on the other hand, with the theological theories (or doctrines) that men have developed to conceptualize the meaning of those encounters. These two components of religion, religious experience and religious beliefs, although distinguishable, are not separable. It is as hard to say which came first as it is in the celebrated case of the hen and the egg. For they continually react upon one another in a joint process of development, experience providing the ground of our beliefs and these in turn influencing the forms taken by our experience. And the different religions are different streams of religious experience, each having started at a different point within human history, and each having formed its own conceptual self-consciousness within a different cultural milieu.

To see the historical inevitability of the plurality of religions in the past, and its non-evitability in the future, we must note the broad course that has been taken by the religious life of mankind. Man has been described as a naturally religious animal. He displays an innate tendency to experience his environment as religiously as well as naturally significant, and to feel required to live in it as such. This tendency is universally expressed in the cultures of primitive man, with his belief in sacred objects, endowed with *Mana*, and in a multitude of spirits needing to be carefully propitiated. The divine reality is here crudely apprehended as a plurality of quasi-animal forces. The next stage seems to have come with the coalescence of tribes into nations. The tribal gods were then ranked into hierarchies (some being amalgamated in the process) dominated by great national gods, such as the Sumerian Ishtar, Amon of Thebes, Jahweh of Israel, Marduk of Babylon, the Greek Zeus, and so on. The world of tribal and national gods, generally martial and cruel and sometimes requiring human sacrifices, reflected the state of man's awareness of the divine at the dawn of documentary history, some three thousand years ago.

So far, the whole development can be described as the growth of natural religion. That is to say, primitive spirit-worship expressing man's fears of the unknown forces of nature in terms of an innate but incohate sense of the divine, and the worship of national deities, symbolizing the solidarity of the community, again in terms of the natural religious tendency of his mind, represent the extent of man's religious life apart from special intrusions of divine revelation or illumination.

But sometime after 1000 B.C., what has been called the golden age of religious creativity dawned. This consisted in a series of revelatory experiences occurring throughout the world, which deepened and purified men's conceptions of the divine, and which religious faith can only attribute to the pressure of the divine reality upon the human spirit. First came the early Jewish prophets, declaring that they had heard the Word of the Lord claiming their obedience and demanding a new level of righteousness and justice in the life of Israel. Then, in Persia, the prophet Zoroaster appeared; Greece produced Pythagoras, and then Socrates and Plato; China produced Lao-tzu and Confucius; and in India the Vedas and Upanishads were written and Gotama the Buddha lived. Then came the writing of the Bhagavad-Gītā in India and, after a short gap, the life of Jesus of Nazareth and the emergence of Christianity; and after another gap, the prophet Muḥammad and the rise of Islam.

It is important to observe the situation within which the revelatory moments occurred. Communication between the different groups of humanity was then so limited that for all practical purposes men inhabited a series of different worlds. For the most part, people in South America, in Europe, in India, in Arabia, in Africa, in China, were each unaware of the others' existence. There was thus, inevitably, a multiplicity of local religions that were also local cultures. Accordingly, the great creative moments of revelation and illumination occurred within different cultures and influenced their development, giving them the coherence and impetus to expand into larger units, thus producing the vast religious-cultural entities that we now call world religions. So it is that in the past the different streams of religious experience and belief have flowed through different cultures, each forming and being formed by its own separate environment. There has of course been contact between different religions at certain points in history, and an influence of one upon another, and indeed sometimes an important influence;

but nevertheless the broad picture is one of religions developing separately within different historical and cultural settings.

It is thus possible to consider the hypothesis that the great religions are all, at their experiential roots, in contact with the same ultimate divine reality, but that their differing experiences of that reality, interacting over the centuries with the different thought forms of different cultures, have led to increasing differentiation and contrasting elaboration – so that Hinduism, for example, is a very different phenomenon from Christianity, and very different ways of conceiving and experiencing the divine occur within them. However, now that, in the 'one world' of today, the religious traditions are consciously interacting with each other in mutual observation and in inter-faith dialogue, it is possible that their future developments may be on gradually converging courses. For during the next few centuries they will no doubt each continue to change, and it may be that they will grow closer together, and even that one day such names as 'Christianity', 'Buddhism', 'Islam', 'Hinduism', will no longer describe the then current configurations of man's religious experience and belief. I am not here thinking of the extinction of human religiousness in a universal secularization. That is of course a possible future; and indeed many think it the most likely future to come about. But if man is an indelibly religious animal he will always, even amidst secularization, experience a sense of the transcendent by which he will be both troubled and uplifted. The future I am thinking of is accordingly one in which what we now call different religions will constitute the past history of different emphases and variations within something that it need not be too misleading to call a single world religion. I do not mean that all men everywhere will be religious, any more than they are today. I mean rather that the discoveries now taking place by men of different faiths of central common ground, hitherto largely concealed by the variety of cultural forms in which it was expressed, may eventually render obsolete the sense of belonging to rival ideological communities. I do not mean that all religious men will think alike, or worship in the same way, or experience the divine identically. On the contrary, so long as there is a rich variety of human cultures – and let us hope that there will always be this – we should expect there to be correspondingly different forms of religious cult, ritual, and organization, conceptualized in different theological doctrines. And so long as there is a wide spectrum of human psychological types – and again let us hope that there will always be this – we should expect there to be correspondingly different emphases between, for example, the sense of the divine as just and as merciful, between *karma* and *bhakti*; or between worship as formal and communal and worship as free and personal. Thus we may expect the different world faiths to continue as religious-cultural phenomena, though phenomena that are increasingly interpenetrating one another. The relation between them will then be somewhat like that now obtaining between the different denominations of Christianity in this country. That is to say, there will in most countries be a dominant religious tradition (as Anglicanism is dominant in England today), with other traditions present in varying strengths, but with considerable awareness on all hands of what they have in common, with osmosis of membership taking place through their institutional walls, with some degree of interchange of ministry and a large degree of practical co-operation.

If the nature of religion, and the history of religions, is indeed such that a development of this kind takes place in the remaining decades of the present century and during the succeeding twenty-first century, what does this imply concerning the problem of the conflicting truth-claims of the different religions in their present forms?

It is, I think, possible to distinguish three aspects of this problem – differences in modes of experience of the divine reality; differences of philosophical and theological theory concerning that reality; and differences in the key, or revelatory, experiences that unify a stream of religious experience and thought.

There are a number of instances of the first kind of difference – for example the contrast between, on the one hand, the experience of God as personal in Judaism, Christianity, Islam, and the strand of Hinduism – according to Santosh Sengupta, in his paper on the 'The Misunderstanding of Hinduism', the major strand – expressed in the thought of the school of Rāmānuja and in the Bhagavad-Gītā, and on the other hand the experience of the divine as non-personal in Advaita Vedānta Hinduism and in Buddhism; or, within theism, the contrast between the experience of God as stern judge and as gracious friend. There is, I think, in principle no difficulty in holding that these pairs can be understood as complementary rather than as rival truths. For if, as every profound form of theism has affirmed, God is infinite, and accordingly exceeds the scope of our finite human categories, He may be both personal lord and impersonal ground of being; both judge and father, source both of justice and of love. This possibility is discussed by Jehangir Chubb in his paper, 'Presuppositions of Inter-Faith Dialogue',[9] in which he speaks of Sri Aurobindo's 'logic of the Infinite', in which different phenomenological characteristics are not mutually exclusive. Here, it appears to me, the way forward is to explore further the special logic of the infinite to which Sri Aurobindo and his school have drawn attention.

The second type of difference is difference in philosophical and theological theory or doctrine. Such differences, and indeed conflicts, do exist and are not merely apparent; but they are part of the still developing history of human thought, and it may be that sooner or later they will be transcended. For they belong to the historical, culturally conditioned aspect of religion, within which any degree of change is possible.

I would offer as a typical example of this second kind of difference the Indian doctrine of reincarnation set over against the Christian doctrine of one life only in this world. Each of these rival theories, it is important to notice, takes several different forms. There is reincarnation, first, as an empirical hypothesis about the rebirth of the conscious, memory-bearing self, this hypothesis being supported by the evidence of individuals who claim to remember a former life. Second, there is reincarnation as a metaphysical theory about a spiritual entity, the higher soul, which lies behind the empirical self but of which this self is not normally conscious. The soul produces a series of selves as its expressions and instruments, these successive selves being described as reincarnations of the same eternal soul. And third, there is reincarnation as a mythological expression of the ethical doctrine of what has been called collective *karma*. And on the Christian side there are the two alternative Augustinian and Irenaean streams of theology, according to the first of which the soul goes at death to heaven, hell, or purgatory; but according to the second of which the soul progresses through other spheres of existence beyond this world towards the final heavenly state. Within both Indian and Christian thought debate is possible, and is taking place, between these different understandings. Within Christianity there is, I believe, a tendency towards the Irenaean type of theology, which is itself foreshadowed, so far as its eschatology is concerned, in the Augustinian-Catholic doctrine of purgatory. The Irenaean eschatology, however, is not incompatible with the third interpretation of the idea of reincarnation, and is readily capable of constructive debate with the first interpretation. For there is a basic agreement between them about the principle of continued responsible life, in which the individual may learn and grow by interacting with human beings in a common environment or series of environments. They differ only as to *where* this continued life is to take place. The Christian belief is that it takes place in other worlds beyond this one. The Hindu belief is that it usually takes place by means of repeated returns to this world. But this difference is relatively slight in comparison with the more fundamental agreement. Indeed the question whether man's continued life takes the form of progress through other spheres, or progress from incarnation to incarnation within this world, would seem to be a matter of probable judgement rather than of essential Christian and Hindu faith respectively. Apart from the weight of tradition behind us, which is of course very liable to predetermine what we think, I see no compelling reason why a Christian should not come to believe in reincarnation instead of in continued life in other spheres, or why a Hindu should not come to believe in continued life on other spheres instead of in reincarnation.

I cannot pursue this particular issue here; I cite it however as an example of a doctrinal clash in which there is room for manoeuvre on both sides, and in which the conditions exist for fruitful dialogue and joint exploration, the final outcome of which might be a transcending of the present conflict of beliefs. I would not however, express this situation, as does Cantwell Smith, by saying that there are here no conflicting truth-claims, but rather that there may at some time in the future, as a result of constructive dialogue, come to be agreement between those who now sponsor these conflicting doctrines.

But it is the third kind of difference that constitutes the largest difficulty in the way of religious agreement. For each religion has its holy founder or scripture, or both, in which the divine reality has been revealed – the Vedas, the Torah, the Buddha, Christ and the Bible, the Qur'ān. And wherever the holy is revealed it claims an absolute response of faith and worship, which thus seems incompatible with a like response to any other disclosure of the holy. In the case of Christianity, this absoluteness of response has been strongly developed in our theology, being conceptually solidified for many centuries by the formulation of the Council of Chalcedon (A.D. 451) that Christ was uniquely divine, being of one substance with God the Father. In modern times, however, the monolithic character of the traditional doctrine of the uniqueness of Christ has been modified in a number of new interpretations of the idea of incarnation – for example, the 'paradox of grace' Christology suggested by the late D. M. Baillie. And in the present volume Kenneth Cragg, in his essay on 'Islam and Incarnation', boldly turns to this most acute of all points of conflict, especially between Islam and Christianity, and in his very careful essay of tentative exploration begins to build a bridge over even this apparently unbridgeable chasm by means of the notion of the divine 'sending' into the human.

We cannot, I think, yet claim to be able to see a way through the obstacle that the traditional doctrine of the incarnation presents to a future global theology. This is the point at which fresh dialogue and fresh exploration are most needed and yet most difficult.[10] It is appropriate, because realistic, to end this essay on this note of mingled doubt and hope. We live amidst unfinished business; but we must trust that continuing dialogue will prove to be dialogue into truth, and that in a fuller grasp of truth our present conflicting doctrines will ultimately be transcended.

NOTES

1 New York, 1964.

2 *Questions of Religious Truth* (Victor Gollancz, 1967) p. 73.

3 *The Imitation of Christ*, I, 3.5.

4 *Questions of Religious Truth*, p. 115.

5 *Ibid.*, p. 68.

6 *Ibid.*, pp. 70-1.

7 *Ibid.*, pp. 89-90.

8 *Ibid.*, p. 94.

9 *Religious Studies*, Vol. 8, No. 4 (Dec. 1972). Dr Chubb's paper was originally presented to the Birmingham Conference in 1970.

10 Since writing this I have attempted to make a contribution to the resolution of this issue in *God and the Universe of Faiths* (Macmillan, 1973) ch. 12.

JOHN HICK is Professor of Theology in the University of Birmingham. Author of *Faith and Knowledge*; *Philosophy of Religion*; *Evil and the God of Love*; *Christianity at the Centre*; *Arguments for the Existence of God*; *Biology and the Soul*; *God and the Universe of Faiths*, etc.

Conflicting Truth-Claims: A Rejoinder

WILFRED CANTWELL SMITH

Our chairman and editor has generously allowed me to submit a note on my reluctance about the formulation 'conflicting truth-claims' for conceptualizing the topic of our conference, and on the fact that my resistance to such wording was not dissipated even when it was modified into 'apparently conflicting truth-claims'. The matter is of some importance, and my dissatisfaction seemed patently bizarre; so that I welcome this opportunity to elucidate the issues as I see them. Implicit are major questions of the relation of philosophical to religious awareness, of West to East, and other great matters.

In the conference itself, when one of our number (from India) affirmed the transmigration of souls and another (from Europe) denied it, their statements surely conflicted, or at least appeared to conflict, it was urged; so that I seemed both obtuse and obdurate when, in the face of this, I still demurred to the formula. My position is a serious one, however: I take the problem of religious diversity with the utmost earnestness and, I like to feel, with deliberate realism. My contention is that the problem can be perceived in more than one way; and that to perceive it in terms of truth-claims that conflict is not necessary, and not necessarily helpful.

At play here is the recognition, that perception is an activity. The comparative history of religion makes unusually evident that man's ways of perceiving the world and each part of it are culturally conditioned, and are saliently consequential. How a problem is perceived is, of course, a highly significant matter for the possible solutions to it that will then be conceived. To perceive this particular problem in this particular manner is, I have learned to feel, to impose upon it an *a priori* interpretation that arises out of past predispositions but is liable to distort what it apprehends and at the very least to make a solution difficult. To concede that the conflict of truth-claims may be apparent rather than real is to suggest one such potential solution, but within the bounds of an assessment of the issues along lines already determined.

A difficulty inherent in this whole operation is, of course, that the great religious positions of mankind are each total *Weltanschauungen* conceptually or symbolically embracing everything: the world, as a whole and in parts, human life, human destiny, good and evil, actuality and potentiality, transcendence and the infinite, truth. They do not, therefore, lend themselves readily, or at all, to being subsumed under or subordinated to any alternative stance. To judge one by the criteria of another is clearly a whit inept. Now I would submit that the Western rational-critical tradition is of the same type, in this regard. It is one of the total systems, among the others. As major, and conceivably as painful, a self-transformation, as radical and as creative a self-reinterpretation, will be required of Western philosophical thought as is being required of, for instance, the Christian world view, once it has recognized itself as one system among others; once it has realized that it cannot embrace other systems (which it calls 'the religions') within itself, may not use its own categories to interpret and to assess all that it encounters; that Western logic is no more universal than Christian theology.

Western thinkers are accustomed to taking the whole universe into their purview, and feel particularly that truth and falsity, logical consistency and incompatibility, are matters that it is their business, and at least ideally their competence or their challenge, to judge. The Western intellect may have begun to feel less ready than it once was to adjudicate whether a statement made within a radically alien universe of discourse is true or false. Yet it still feels uneasy at any suspicion that it cannot assess whether two statements, even within that alien universe, and perhaps even from two separate such universes, are logically compatible or not.

I, too, am uneasy at unresolved pluralism, and will not acquiesce in that sort of systems-relevatism that recognizes truth and falsity, reality and unreality, and the rest as legitimate questions within each rounded whole but sees the several wholes as independent and mutually exclusive – although I feel the force of this, and as an historian observe that our world has proceeded in roughly that fashion until yesterday. I feel that we have yet to hammer out, collaboratively among men of our varying systems, a new vision that will eventually enable us to embrace not only the universe, as we have each more or less done, but also each other's views of the universe, as we must next do. Meanwhile no one of us, of any cultural or religious or philosophical stance, is quite in a position yet to pass verdicts either on the others of us or on the relations among us. This we must struggle and strive to be able some day to do, as I guess most of us recognize; and it will involve, as we have hardly yet recognized, the construction of new categories, in terms of which to think about these problems, and as well of new attitudes with which to approach them.

In general, then, when a Hindu and a Christian, let us say, make different statements, neither of them, nor a Western secularist listening in, is in a position hastily to determine whether they agree or disagree. Each statement is made within a total world view; the meaning of each term of each, as well as of each whole, derives from the total complex of which it is a more or less coherent part; the function of religious statements within each system is itself particular. The totality within which it obtains not only confers the meaning upon each term within the statement, and upon the statement as a whole, but determines also 'the meaning of meaning' for such statements.

More specifically, let us look at the particulars of our proposed formula. I am ill at ease, first, with the notion of 'truth-claims'. This unhappy neologism is part of the armoury used in the attack by analytic philosophers upon religious statements generally. It distorts, I venture to suggest. When a religious man makes a statement, especially of the 'I believe' sort, and is then asked (more or less peremptorily), 'Do you claim that that is true?' he probably answers 'Yes' – poor chap: what else can he do? (The question is of the 'Have you stopped beating your wife?' sort, although not obviously.) Yet the original statement was not put forth as a 'claim'; and to dub it so is insensitive at best. Especially in so far as religious affirmations are, as perhaps the best of them are, either the asseverations of saints or the interpretations of these by theologians, they are not primarily claims, since sensitive religious persons do not go around making claims. The term is altogether too pretentious.

I much prefer, for example, the standard Islamic notion, of bearing witness. As I have annotated elsewhere, Muslims do not 'claim' that there is no god but God, nor that Muḥammad is His prophet. Rather, they 'bear witness to' these truths (to these 'truths'). Would our conference, and the history of recent Western philosophy generally, not have had a different tone if the formulation of its problem were in terms of divergent witness-bearing?

There are a number of further alternatives. The early Christian movement was launched in terms not of 'claiming' a truth but of proclaiming, heralding (κηρυξ), good news. Why not a conference on the diversity of good news among religious groups?

Hindu scriptural statements are traditionally divided into those that have been heard and those that have been remembered. Other enunciations are of what men have seen, have experienced. In general, Hindu and many other religious statements may better be characterized as 'reports'. Would it not be more gentle, more reminiscent of that renowned elephant, more compassionate to those of us who are blind as we touch it, if a conference were on varying truth reports?

To 'claim' to 'have' the 'truth' is the posture of those who act as if they had God in their pockets – a posture of lesser men not unknown, alas, in religious history but far from the best or most authentic representatives of any tradition. Religious statements at their best (and is it the purpose to deal with them at any lower level?) have been expressions of personal or corporate involvements, tentative but joyous, inadequate but exhuberant, human but transcendence-oriented. To approach them with sympathy is to hear them not as claims but as echoes, to see them not as the moon but as fingers pointing to the moon.

(This sort of consideration is the more poignant for those of us who have observed an historical counterpart in the case not of philosophers accosting the religious but of one religious group assaulting another. Historically, a decisive turning point was attained when, to cite one example that I happen to have studied, Christian missionaries and scholars of Islamics moved beyond the stage of formally criticizing Muslim articulations, demanding of them that they stand up to [sc. alien] analysis and asking peremptorily whether they made sense [sc. to an outsider], and began instead, with the assumption that they manifestly made sense [to intelligent insiders], to ask what steps the outsider could take so as to appreciate that sense and to apprehend the insider's meaning. The former stage proved much less fruitful; the latter's fruitfulness is being harvested sufficiently richly to illustrate that, across cultural and religious boundaries, understanding is in significant part a function of orientation and attitudinal approach.)

If, then, the notion of 'truth-claim' bristles, tends to impose interpretations and perhaps to distort, how much added belligerence is potentially provided by the interpretation 'conflicting'. Divergence, perhaps. Difference, certainly. But to see difference as conflict is to perceive things in a particular way. Tschaikovsky is radically different from Bach; whether they conflict or not is a judgement. Some Catholics may feel, and even say, that Rome is the centre of the world, some Muslims that Makkah is, some scientists that Greenwich is. Muslims and Hindus, with their profoundly differing religious orientations, have lived in India sometimes at peace, sometimes in conflict; are we to assert that when they have fought each other they have been right, and when they have lived juxtaposed or in harmony or complementarily, they have somehow erred?

To see difference as conflict is a decision – whether taken consciously or unconsciously. Admittedly, the Western tradition – *teste* the Crusades, the Thirty Years' War – has tended to make such a decision until recently, and the intellectual tradition has tended to perpetuate it, no doubt unconsciously: if two people, or two statements, disagree, let's battle it out. With a different prior orientation, however, it is both theoretically and practically possible to see two differing statements as an invitation to synthesis rather than a challenge to confrontation.

Hence my unresponsiveness to the offer of allowing that the conflict may be only apparent. One does not in fact know that in the end the conflict may not be real; but in the meantime what appears is not conflict but difference. It may be interpreted, if we choose, not as the threat of diminution but as the promise of enlargement. The perception of conflict in the present situation, of a pluralism just beginning to become self-conscious, is an unwarranted prior judgement as to what the outcome will eventually be, and an unkind prior decision as to what our mood be now. To choose polemics rather than irenics at the present stage of our new encounter with each other – even in surreptitious theory – is unnecessary and, surely, unwise. To insist on seeing conflict whenever one finds, in fundamentally differing systems, two statements of which a person would not make both within one of those systems or in a third, is unduly embattled, beleaguered.

Lest it be felt that my position is in danger of being merely sentimental, polly-anna-ish, let me illustrate the thesis concretely, however inadequately. First, my contention that divergence of statements may be seen as an invitation to synthesis may be evidenced by the endeavour, in *Questions of Religious Truth*, to come to grips with the two traditional answers to the major question, Is the Qur'ān the Word of God? I have by no means sought to evade the challenging persistence of the polarity of answers; many years of wrestling went into the proffered solution, which may not itself have carried conviction but at least perhaps showed the kind of thing that can be done or that needs doing. Similarly the quite different divergence that came up at our conference: an Indian saying that he believed in the transmigration of souls and a Christian saying that he did not. On this I have not pondered for years, and I have no reason to suppose that the truth(s?) to which each presumably or conceivably bears witness can be synthesized easily or will be soon; although I should find it not foolish to imagine that within, let us say, twenty-five years a satisfactory synthesis might well be forthcoming. In the meantime I could mention the lines upon which if it were my task I should begin to ponder; others would doubtless proceed differently.

First, the notion 'soul' presumably has differing meanings in the Indian and the Christian traditions. (The fact that Indian Buddhists could believe in transmigration without believing in souls suggests some of the potential complexities here.)

Secondly, 'I believe' also has different meanings in the two traditions, although the fact that the positive statement on transmigration was made by an Indian authority on Western philosophy would modify this somewhat.

Thirdly, it seems to me evident that both the notion of transmigration and the Christian doctrine of either an immortal soul or resurrection or of some intermingling of the two are metaphors in some sense. (No doubt the concept of metaphor, and its use in either tradition historically, and in both since the rise of science and of positivist philosophies, themselves raise highly intricate questions. Yet neither theory can be or would wish to be 'literally' true in several senses of the word 'literal'.)

Finally, it seems to me extremely probable that there is a quality or dimension to every human life transcending man's immediate mundane historical existence, transcending the spatio-temporal, to which both the traditional Christian and the traditional Indian doctrine give intellectually inadequate and yet not illegitimate expression. The role of religious symbols is to say something that cannot be said otherwise (or has not yet been said otherwise: the rationalist tradition has not yet adequately formulated that quality or dimension of our life; some day perhaps it will?).

The two statements certainly differ; to me they do not appear to conflict.

And, to conclude: may we not perhaps come nearer the truth – who is God – if we do not claim it, but recognize rather, in humility, that we are claimed by it, and are inspired by it, so as to strive onwards towards constantly closer approximations, excited and delighted that nowadays our intellectual apprehensions are being enlarged and deepened in the dialectic of our broadening and tantalizingly variegated community?

Index